Real Kids

Real Stories

Real Character

Choices That Matter
Around the World

Garth Sundem

free spirit
PUBLISHING®

Library of Congress Cataloging-in-Publication Data
Names: Sundem, Garth, author.
Title: Real kids, real stories, real character : choices that matter around the world / Garth Sundem.
Description: Golden Valley, MN : Free Spirit Publishing, [2016] | Includes index.
Identifiers: LCCN 2016016029 (print) | LCCN 2016025225 (ebook) | ISBN 9781631980268 (paperback) | ISBN 1631980262 (paperback) | ISBN 9781631981265 (Web pdf) | ISBN 9781631981272 (Epub)
Subjects: LCSH: Children—Biography—Anecdotes—Juvenile literature. | Children—Conduct of life—Anecdotes—Juvenile literature. | Courage—Anecdotes—Juvenile literature. | Creative ability—Anecdotes—Juvenile literature. | Diligence—Anecdotes—Juvenile literature. | Children—Political activity—Anecdotes—Juvenile literature. | Social action—Anecdotes— Juvenile literature. | Altruism in children—Anecdotes—Juvenile literature. | BISAC: JUVENILE NONFICTION / Social Issues / Values & Virtues. | JUVENILE NONFICTION / Social Issues / Self-Esteem & Self-Reliance.
Classification: LCC CT107 .S7983 2016 (print) | LCC CT107 (ebook) | DDC 305.23—dc23
LC record available at https://lccn.loc.gov/2016016029

Cover photo credits, top to bottom: AP Photo/Marcio Jose Sanchez; AP Photo/Judy Fitzpatrick, File; AP Photo/Grant Hindsley

Reading Level Grade 6; Interest Level Ages 9–13
Fountas & Pinnell Guided Reading Level W

Edited by Brian Farrey-Latz
Cover and interior design by Colleen Rollins

10 9 8 7 6 5 4 3 2 1
Printed in the United States of America
V20300616

Free Spirit Publishing Inc.
6325 Sandburg Road, Suite 100
Minneapolis, MN 55427-3674
(612) 338-2068
help4kids@freespirit.com
www.freespirit.com

To Leif and Kess,
may you change the world.

CONTENTS

Justice was the star wide receiver of his middle school football team. When the team engineered a way for their learning disabled team manager to score a touchdown, they all had the opportunity to be famous. Here's what Justice did instead.

Chapter 4: Persistence and Grit 84

It took 14-year-old Robert hundreds of hours at the public library to learn to design the game app Bubble Ball. Now, it's been downloaded over 9 million times.

Is your lunchroom a little bit gray, a little bit dark . . . a little bit drab? It sure was at Brooklyn's PS 123. Christopher decided to do something about it.

Was that a dog in an open garage on a freezing Michigan night? The back of 10-year-old Danny DiPietro's mind told him it was something more, and he didn't give up until his mom went to check it out.

What do you get when you spend thousands of hours taking hundreds of runs on a small, icy ski hill in New Hampshire? Perfect technique, that's what. Oh, and some Olympic medals.

Chapter 5: Resilience 102

Chapter 6: Responsibility

William Kamkwamba: Tower of Power (Malawi)

Who makes sure your electricity stays on? In the African country of Malawi, 13-year-old William decided he would do it himself.

Laura Dekker: Around the World in 519 Days (The Netherlands)

Anchors away! Hoist the storm jib! Wait, take down the storm jib! Oh no, it's jammed! On her solo sail around the world, Laura had to save herself.

Diane Tran: Jailed for Responsibility (Texas)

Seventeen-year-old Diane Tran was an honors student working two after-school jobs to support her brother and sister. This is why she went to jail.

Sarbast Ali: A School of One (Iraq)

Sarbast was in a wheelchair and couldn't get to school over the rough ground in the Domiz refugee camp in Northern Iraq. That's why Sarbast took his education into his own hands.

INTRODUCTION

How tall are you? How athletic are you? How smart are you and how many friends do you have? How much money do you have and where do you live? What music do you like and what clothes do you wear? What language do you speak at home? The answers to these questions shape the story you tell yourself about who you are—they help you understand your *identity*.

These questions are also pretty easy to answer. You're either five feet tall or you're not. You either like classical music or you don't. This layer of your identity is like the paint on a house—it's either red or it's not. But what goes on inside that house is a whole other story, and the questions that shape your inside story are much harder to answer:

If you see a friend doing something you know is wrong, do you speak up? If you mess up on the sports field or on a test, does it make you quit or does it push you to practice harder? When you see a problem in the world, do you wait for others to figure it out or do you search for your own solutions? If you were diagnosed with a life-changing disease, would you still show the world your smile? When you do a good deed, do you need people to know about it?

When you think about things like courage, kindness, creativity, persistence, resilience, and responsibility—

some of the things that make up your *character*—it's pretty easy to imagine you're like the person you heard about who saved someone from the subway tracks and think you'd do the same! But would you? Would you *really?* Unless you've been put to the test, you might not know.

It's hard to know your character. It's also hard to change it. Doing one brave thing doesn't necessarily make you courageous, just like doing one kind thing doesn't necessarily make you a kind person. The opposite is true, too: Just because you came home from soccer practice one afternoon and said something mean to your little brother or sister doesn't make you a spineless jellyfish toad who should start sleeping in the garage to protect humanity from your evil.

Character is not necessarily something you learn with your head—it's something you feel with your heart. You can try studying it like you study for a math test, but that's about as good as trying to eat peas with a knife. Being able to define character isn't the same thing as having it.

If you really want to know and grow character, you have to experience it. You have to see it in action. You have to sit with character until it finds its way into your head *and your heart.* This book is a good start. But even at its best, it's just a start. When the bell rings or you close this book for the night, that's when character really starts. That's when you have the chance to *actually be* one of the young people from these pages.

It doesn't take a million dollars or a superpower to have character. It just takes a choice—the choice to be conscious of your choices. The choice to do the best you can do in your imperfect skin with your imperfect brain in an imperfect world. In some ways, it's the choice to *matter*. And in some ways, it's the choice to let other people matter more. These choices, over the course of your life, make up your character. These choices start today.

Garth Sundem

Chapter 1

Courage

Courage is saving a kitten that's stuck in a tall tree. But it's also so much more. Courage is the willingness to do something difficult. Maybe it takes two seconds, like telling a friend to stop bullying. Or maybe courage happens over years and years, like living a positive life with a challenging health condition. It can be something you do with your body, like saving the kitten. Or it can be something you do with your heart and your mind, like choosing to speak out against injustice. It can also take courage to *avoid* something, like following friends or family members into activities you know would be bad for you.

No matter what form it takes, courage is the force that changes the natural direction of things. If you don't show courage, things just . . . continue. The kitten remains in danger, injustice goes on and on, or you end up doing what's easy instead of what's right.

Courage isn't easy. But it's what makes impossible things possible. What do you think is possible? Why not find out?

The Courage to Be Different
Zach Veach

When Zach Veach was four years old, he told his parents he wanted to be a professional racecar driver. It made sense: Zach grew up watching his dad, Roger, drive in truck and tractor pull competitions. But his family knew how much work it takes to become a pro driver and only wanted Zach to go down that long road if it was what he really, really wanted. When other kids in his small hometown of Stockdale, Ohio, started racing go-karts, the first step on the long path to driving professionally, Zach's parents encouraged him to wait.

Then when Zach was 11, his dad won the national truck and tractor pull championship in Macon, Missouri.

"Driving home from the championship, we saw a little go-kart track off the highway," Zach says. They pulled over, and there on the side of the road, Zach got his first taste behind the wheel. "I don't know why, but that day my dad decided to sell his trucks and tractors, give it all up, and help me reach my dream."

Zach's dad bought him a go-kart, and Zach started going to the local track after school and on weekends, running endless laps alone late into the evenings to get a feel for what a kart could and couldn't do. People have called Zach a "natural." But this "natural" talent actually came from sacrificing every evening and weekend to get thousands of hours of practice.

With practice, Zach started to get fast.

Really fast.

So fast that his lap times started to turn heads. One of those heads was famous racecar driver Michael Andretti, who owned an IndyCar team. After watching 14-year-old Zach drive, Andretti invited him to try out for his USF2000 team, which is kind of like what college baseball is to the minors. It was Zach's first taste of professional racing, and he ate it up, finishing fifth in points despite starting after the first two races of the season had already been run. In 2010, Zach was a semi-finalist for *Sports Illustrated Kids* SportsKid of the Year.

FAST FACTS

IndyCar is a professional auto-racing organization.

But Zach's skills on the racetrack didn't matter back at his middle school in Stockdale. Because Zach was small, he was picked on at school. Once, a kid pushed his head down onto a desk so hard that Zach chipped a tooth. Another time, Zach won a weekend race in Indiana and proudly wore the winner's cap to school on Monday. At lunch, a kid grabbed the hat, poured milk on it, and threw it in a trashcan. Zach took it in stride. When winners of the Indianapolis 500 cross the finish line, they're handed a bottle of milk and they pour it over themselves. Zach retrieved his hat and imagined he had just won the famous race.

When Zach was 15, he graduated to the Indy Light circuit—like minor league baseball and just one step away from the major leagues of IndyCar itself. In Indy Light, Zach would be driving at about 200 miles per hour, and he was still too young to get a driver's license!

It was pretty obvious some of the older drivers didn't think Zach belonged. He'd be on the inside of a turn and an experienced driver would push him into the grass. It felt like having his face shoved into a desk by a kid at school or having his hat thrown in the trashcan all over again. Maybe at school he was too small to be a match for the kids who bullied him, but behind the wheel, the size of his body didn't matter— it was his courage that counted. For Zach, courage was all about finding a peaceful mind.

"Driving is one of the most peaceful places on earth," he says. "You have to get into your mindset. Even when people are trying to shove you around, you have to stay cool and confident so you don't make mistakes."

On the track, Zach let his driving do the talking. His first year in Indy Light, he took third in a race at the Milwaukee Mile and won a race at Auto Club Speedway in Fontana, California, to finish the season in seventh place overall. In 2014, Zach's second Indy Lights season, he won three races and stood on the podium nine times to finish third overall.

"Ever since I was young, I was that kid climbing trees, wanting to know how high I could get. I've always been interested in finding my limits, pushing myself to see how far I could take myself," Zach says. For Zach, courage has always meant more than going 250 miles per hour while inches away from other cars going just as fast. It's been the courage to be different, the courage to find his limits.

OHIO, USA
population: 11.6 million
capital: Columbus

Now at age 21, Zach is trying to race in the big leagues: the IndyCar circuit. By the time you're reading this book, all it will take is a quick Google search to see if he made it. Whether the answer is yes or no, you can bet that Zach had the courage to *try*.

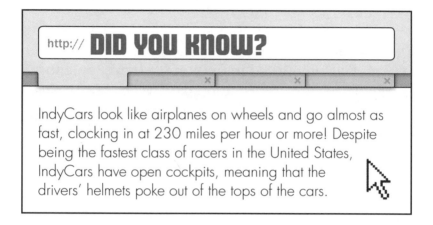

http:// **DID YOU KNOW?**

IndyCars look like airplanes on wheels and go almost as fast, clocking in at 230 miles per hour or more! Despite being the fastest class of racers in the United States, IndyCars have open cockpits, meaning that the drivers' helmets poke out of the tops of the cars.

To Educate a Girl Is to Educate a Nation
Eunice Muba

Imagine the city of Los Angeles. Now, shrink the size of the city and double the population. Double the murder rate. Turn up the temperature. Take all the money in the city and divide it into 100 bags. Throw 99 of these bags into the ocean. Finally, scoop some money out of that final bag. Throw that in the ocean, too. That's what it's like in the city of Kinshasa, the capital of the Democratic Republic of the Congo—the "DRC"—in Africa.

In the DRC, if you speak out against the govern-ment, you could be beaten up or thrown in jail. But that's nothing compared to speaking out against the armed rebel groups like the Lord's Resistance Army, M23, and the Interahamwe. *That* can get you killed. But how can you *not* speak out? In Kinshasa, almost 14,000 kids live on the streets, and in the eastern part of the country, the rebel groups kidnap young people and force them to fight in their armies.

In many places around the world, protections guarantee that journalists can speak freely and write the truth. That's not necessarily true in the DRC. In the DRC, many reporters are told what to write and what not to write. But Franck Kangundu, a reporter for the newspaper *La Référence Plus*, didn't play by that rule. He wrote critically about the government and business. On November 3, 2005, men in black masks burst into his home and shot Franck and his wife to death. If you were scared for your life and the lives of the people you love, would you write important stories

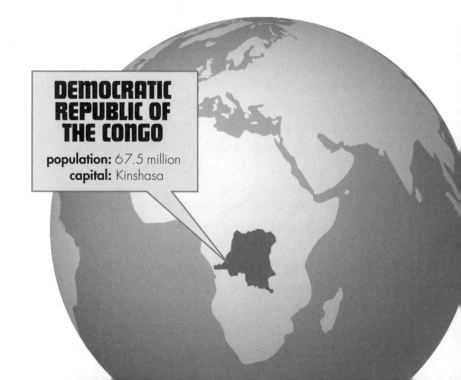

DEMOCRATIC REPUBLIC OF THE CONGO

population: 67.5 million
capital: Kinshasa

about corrupt people in government and business, or would you write about the things that powerful people told you to write?

That is the dilemma of Eunice Muba, a teenage reporter for the website Ponabana, which is a mouth-piece for human rights managed by the international aid organization UNICEF. Eunice writes articles demanding more rights for girls in the DRC. In the Democratic Republic of the Congo, three out of four girls are married before age 18. And while three out of four girls go to primary school, only one out of four girls goes to high school.

"Girls are hindered by so many obstacles, such as the belief that only boys should go to school and that it is not necessary to invest in girls' education," writes Eunice.

"Many Congolese children are in poor living conditions, especially in terms of access to healthcare services, and I hope to be able to write about this or talk about what I am doing in my school so that my schoolmates can learn more about their rights," Eunice writes.

In 2012, Eunice traveled to Addis Ababa, the capital of Ethiopia, to speak to world leaders at the Convention on the Rights of the Child.

"A majority of African children are still exposed to economic exploitation, child labor, lack of education, early marriages, sexual violence, prostitution, ill treatment, drug abuse, and forced recruitment into armed forces. Children are also exposed to diseases such as malaria, cholera, HIV/AIDS, and polio; non-access to safe water; and non-vaccination," she said. And Eunice talked about the importance of protecting children in the DRC from armed conflict in the rural areas and government abuse in the cities.

In 2014, her article "To Educate a Girl Is to Educate a Nation" won the award for best story of the year at the Ponabana website. Writing about her article, Eunice says, "I hope to have brought something to your way of thinking about girls' education and to have allowed more girls to attend school." So far, Eunice has managed to stay safe.

Think about it: You can probably remember a day when you woke up early in the morning and didn't want to go to school. Maybe you can remember even more than one? In countries like the Democratic Republic of the Congo, it is only because people like Eunice have the courage to speak up that children, and especially girls, have the right to go to school at all.

http:// **DID YOU KNOW?**

Go to ponabana.com to read what other brave reporters like Eunice are writing about human rights in the Democratic Republic of the Congo.

Born to Run, Learning to Fly

Winter Vinecki

Have you ever wanted to run and run? At first it feels great, sailing over the cement or along the ribbon of a trail. Eventually, your body starts to hurt. Then you run some more. And when you finally cross the finish line, you discover that you can make it through. You learn that your body can do it. Your mind can do it. You know something about yourself that you can't discover any other way: You're strong enough to survive.

Winter Vinecki had been running races with her parents since she was five and she loved the feeling of pushing her limits with them by her side. But when she was nine years old, her father was diagnosed with a rare kind of prostate cancer. By the time she turned 10, he was gone. Winter's dad passed away when he was only 40 years old.

After her dad died, Winter set the goal of running a marathon on every continent before she turned 15 to honor his memory. There are seven continents. Winter ran the Eugene Marathon in Oregon (North America). She ran the Amazing Maasai Marathon in Kenya (Africa). Then it was time to turn her attention to a marathon on the planet's most inhospitable continent: Antarctica. Maybe you've seen nature shows of penguins huddling together in big groups so they don't freeze to death? Yeah, we're talking about *that* Antarctica.

As you can probably guess, not many people live in Antarctica, where even in summer the average temperature is just a couple degrees above freezing. Most of the people in Antarctica aren't there for fun. They live in military outposts and research stations. The Antarctica Marathon starts and finishes at a small Russian military base. Most marathons have aid stations where lines of volunteers pass out water and energy bars. In the Antarctica Marathon, the aid stations are at tiny military bases run by Uruguay, Chile, and China.

Maybe it helped to have the name "Winter." She ran the course in 4 hours and 49 minutes and was the third female of any age to cross the finish line.

But Winter wasn't done. She ran the Inca Trail Marathon to Machu Picchu (South America), setting a course record at just over 9 hours. She ran the Sunrise to Sunset Marathon in Mongolia (Asia). And she ran the Great Barrier Island Wharf to Wharf Marathon in New Zealand (which she counted as Australia).

Winter's birthday is in December. In the November before her 15th birthday—just in time to reach the goal she set for herself when her dad died—she and her mom ran the Athens Classic Marathon in Greece (Europe). As she crossed the finish line in the Olympic stadium, she said out loud, "This is for you, Dad."

Winter is the youngest person to run marathons on every continent. She ran every race with her mom, and they are also the only mother-daughter team to complete the full tour. Along the way, Team Winter raised over $400,000 for prostate cancer research.

ANTARCTICA

population: 4,000 in summer
1,000 in winter

If you've ever run a long race, you know the pain is different than scraping your knee or closing a car door on your finger. Your body starts to feel like an empty pitcher of water, every last drop poured out . . . and still, you have to find the courage to keep going. After seven marathons on seven continents, Winter had not only poured out her body's energy, but she had poured out the pain, anger, and injustice she felt after her father's death. Winter had met her goal: She had successfully honored her father's life.

After running and running and running through the pain of her loss, Winter switched her focus from marathons to aerial ski jumping. She now lives in Park City, Utah, where she has her sights set on making the U.S. National Team and maybe, someday, the Olympics.

After finding the courage to run, now Winter is learning to fly.

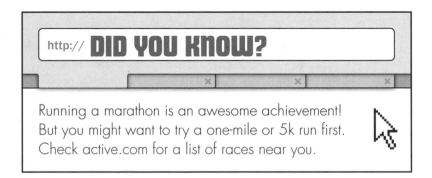

http:// **DID YOU KNOW?**

Running a marathon is an awesome achievement! But you might want to try a one-mile or 5k run first. Check active.com for a list of races near you.

"Caste"-ing Off
Arti Verma

The village of Raiwana in northern India is home
to about 2,000 people. Most of the houses are small,
made of bamboo walls smeared with mud and roofs
thatched with reeds. Surrounding the village is a
patchwork of fields where farmers grow rice, beans,
cotton, and other crops. In the center is the village
chopal, a two-story cement building with colorful balconies, where the village's men gather in the evenings
to socialize.

Life in Raiwana is built on traditions established
hundreds and even thousands of years ago. Some of
these traditions are beautiful, like the five-day festival
of lights known as *Diwali* and the spring festival of
colors and love known as *Holi*. Other traditions are
a little less beautiful. For example, one tradition in
India is that people are divided into "castes." There
are high castes and low castes. Traditionally, people in

high castes are educated and own land. People in low castes are less educated and do the dirty work, especially working with animals, which people of higher castes consider unclean. The people in the lowest caste are known as *dalit,* or "untouchables." And being *dalit* has nothing to do with what is inside of you—if your parents are *dalit,* then you are, too. Though it has been illegal to discriminate against people in the *dalit* caste since 1949, much of Indian society is still segregated and discrimination against *dalit* people is widespread.

Arti Verma was 10 years old and a class V student at a special school that provided free education to children in rural India. That is, the school provided free education to students who were not from the *dalit* caste.

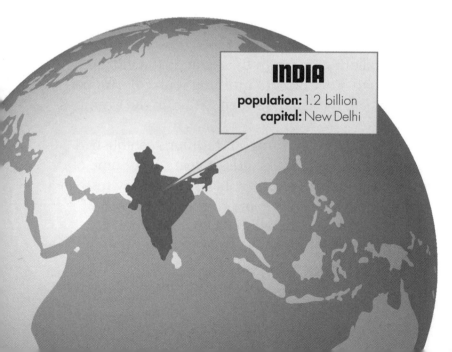

INDIA
population: 1.2 billion
capital: New Delhi

Arti was not from a *dalit* family. Her father was the head of the village. Still, she knew what it was like to feel like a second-class citizen and to be pressured to quit school. In Raiwana and many villages throughout India, girls are expected to work at home with their mothers while boys go to school. Where Arti lived in the state of Rajasthan, only one in every five women could read.

Men from high castes, like Arti's father, had education, land, jobs, money, and power. People from lower castes—especially women and girls struggled to live. Of course, many men from high castes *liked* the caste system, even if they didn't say it out loud. That's because the caste system kept them in power. Because *dalit* people feared violence and weren't allowed to enter the village *chopal* where most decisions were made, they couldn't do much about the system.

But there was something Arti could do. Starting in her school, Arti spoke out against the caste system. She started making posters about the rights of people in lower castes, and she hung the posters around her village. Not everybody was happy with Arti's posters, but despite the danger and disapproval, Arti kept at it. She organized rallies where the *dalit* people of the village and surrounding areas got together to demand their rights.

The men who gathered in the *chopal* didn't care. The *dalit* people could gather. They could make noise. A girl could hang posters. But what difference could the rallies and posters make, really? In the evenings, on the colorful balconies of the *chopal*, the high caste men of Raiwana lived a world apart from the struggle for *dalit* rights and Arti's work.

But slowly, Arti was changing the mind of the person who mattered most: her father. He saw his daughter's determination. He saw the danger that Arti put herself in every day, trying to take power away from powerful people. And through his daughter's eyes, Arti's father started to see *dalit* people in the community as more than "untouchables." He brought his change of heart with him to the *chopal*—to his friends and the other men who ran the community.

In India, laws have been powerless to change the caste system. No one can wave a magic wand and make discrimination and caste violence go away. It takes a friend, a neighbor, sometimes a *daughter*, to make change.

When Arti graduated from class V to class VI, she had a handful of new classmates: the children of *dalit* families in the community. And by the end of that year, with Arti's father now pushing for *dalit* rights in the village's hall of power, *dalit* men were allowed into the *chopal* for the first time. There is still a long way to go for the rights of people in lower castes and women in India, especially in the small villages and rural areas. But because Arti decided to stand up and point her finger at injustice, her little corner of the world is a little fairer.

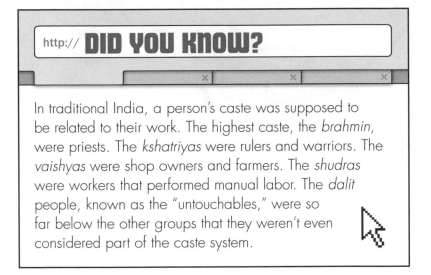

In traditional India, a person's caste was supposed to be related to their work. The highest caste, the *brahmin*, were priests. The *kshatriyas* were rulers and warriors. The *vaishyas* were shop owners and farmers. The *shudras* were workers that performed manual labor. The *dalit* people, known as the "untouchables," were so far below the other groups that they weren't even considered part of the caste system.

Fully Committed
Tom Schaar

"At some point you just tune everything out and say 'this is it,'" says skateboarder Tony Hawk in a video of the 1999 Summer X Games.

That day at the X Games, with the sun going down and the stadium lights high above him, Tony Hawk dropped in to the giant halfpipe. He pumped for speed, launched once, launched twice, and then spun. The stadium held its breath—Hawk had already taken about a dozen hard crashes trying the trick. One. Two. Two and a half rotations! Tony Hawk landed, crouched on his board, and the stadium erupted! He had landed the world's first 900 on a skateboard: 360, 360, and another

24

180! You could see on his face that it was the achievement of his life.

That year, as Tony Hawk reached his ultimate triumph, another skateboarder was born: Tom Schaar of Malibu, California. Tom started skating at age four. Of course, he grew up knowing the story of Tony Hawk landing a 900 at the X Games. Everyone in the sport was wondering: Who's going to beat that? Who's going to go even farther?

Tom remembers going to a Vans Skatepark in Orange County, California, when he was seven. He stood at the top of the 12-foot halfpipe and hung his board over the edge. He'd never dropped in before. A halfpipe isn't something you can do *halfway*. You have to step out into space and come down hard enough on the nose of the board to go vertical with the top of the ramp. If you chicken out and lean back, the board goes flying out forward and you come down on your shorts. Lean too far forward, and you go over the front of the board and your face gets up close and personal with the ramp.

FAST FACTS

Dropping in to a halfpipe means riding your skateboard from the top of one side, straight down the vertical section at the top, and into the halfpipe's "U." Wear your helmet!

"When you're seven, it's scary to look over the edge of a halfpipe. At first you're like panicking," Tom says. Not everybody is a skateboarder, but even if you don't ride, you probably know the feeling: You're staring over the edge of *something*. Once you start, there's no going back. You have to find the courage to commit.

That day at the Orange County halfpipe, Tom dug deep and dropped in. And he fell. Hard. Even when you find the courage to dig deep and commit, sometimes you end up smearing your cheek against the hard plywood of a skateboard ramp.

"After I finished crying, I got up and tried again," Tom says. It took many tries and many falls, but when Tom finally dropped in without splatting, he says it "felt like flying!"

CALIFORNIA, USA

population: 39.1 million
capital: Sacramento

There are more than 5,000 skateparks in the United States. You can bet that at every one of them, people are dropping in to halfpipes and ramps every day. But not many of these skateparks have something like the Mega Ramp at Woodward West Camp in Tehachapi, California, about two hours north of Tom's house in Malibu. The Mega Ramp is a monster—the Godzilla of skate ramps. It starts with a 150-foot ramp that looks like the takeoff for an Olympic ski jump. Then, there's a small hill in the middle. You go up one side, fly 70 feet through the air over a flat section at the top of the hill, and come down smoothly on the hill's downslope, just in time to hit the 27-foot quarter pipe at the end of the Mega Ramp. By that point, you're going more than 35 miles per hour.

"You go, like, 20 feet off the top of the quarter pipe, so at the top you're almost 50 feet in the air," Tom says.

One of the worst things he's seen is people who try the Mega Ramp for the first time and chicken out just as they start up the first gentle hill.

"They figure out at the last second they shouldn't be doing it and try to bail out right before the bulge. They knee slide and end up going over anyway, into the air. But then they don't have enough speed to clear the flat section on the top. It usually doesn't end well. It's bad," he says.

Here's another thing about courage: Sometimes fear is your body's way of saying you're just not quite ready yet. It took Tom a couple years to work up the courage to try the Mega Ramp. "That's probably a good thing," he says.

But by October 2011, a month after he turned 12 years old, Tom had skated the ramp many times (maybe "flown" the ramp is a better way of saying it . . .), and that month he landed a 900, matching Tony Hawk's record. By then, seven other skaters had landed the 900, and a couple skaters had even tried to go further. Tom Schaar had watched from the stands as skateboarder and Olympic snowboarder Shaun White fell 21 times trying to land a 1080 at the X Games in Long Beach, California.

"After landing the 900, I started joking around about the 1080," Tom says. Then he started thinking about it more seriously. After thinking, Tom started training. He'd never practiced on a trampoline before, but he knew that for the 1080 he would have to do something special. He spent hours and hours on trampolines doing spins, "just trying to get the feel of it," he says.

In March 2012, Tom felt ready. It was the same feeling he'd had when he knew it was time to drop in to the 12-foot ramp at the Vans Skatepark in Orange County—the same feeling as knowing that he was ready to ride the Mega Ramp or committing to landing the 900. Tom was ready for the 1080.

"When you're committed, it's terrifying," he says. "All these things are going through your mind. All the things that could go wrong. But then you're also thinking about all the things that could go *right*. It's really scary to commit to any trick, whether it's a really little trick or something big. Then, in the moment, you just think, *I can do this.* And you just go for it."

No one had ever landed a 1080. Not professional skaters in their 20s. Not Shaun White. Not even Tony Hawk. On his first try, Tom lost his board at the top of his air. In a YouTube video, you can see the board spin through the sky 15 feet above the ramp before clacking sideways into the coping at the lip of the ramp. Tom lands on his kneepads and slides down the ramp, his board spinning down after him. It's hard not to imagine what would have happened if it were Tom and not his board that had come down sideways on the hard edge of the giant ramp.

Tom fell four times.

"Skateboarding is fun. It will be fun forever, every time I step on a board. But it's also more than that," Tom says. "It's trying to progress the sport. It's knowing what people have done before you and trying to push forward into what's next."

On his fifth try, Tom came down smooth as butter. Not a wobble. Dead straight. After spinning three full times, falling 15 feet out of the air, and landing on the face of the 27-foot Mega Ramp, he skated out of it rock solid as if he were riding down the sidewalk.

Tony Hawk pioneered the 540, 720, and 900. 12-year-old Tom Schaar brought the 1080 to skating. What's next? Well, what's next is the 1260. "It's so hard for me to imagine more," Tom says. "But I'm sure someone will do it . . . eventually."

Maybe it will be Tom.

Maybe it will be you.

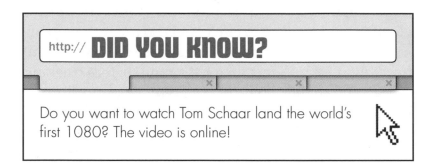

Do you want to watch Tom Schaar land the world's first 1080? The video is online!

How to Hotwire a Truck Radio

Michael Bowron

On October 10, 2009, eight-year-old Michael Bowron was in the sleeper cabin of his dad's semi-truck as they drove home from the family's farm fields in Western Australia. They were on a dusty country road that ran through wheat fields, the only vehicle for miles and miles. That's when the left-front tire blew.

"The truck was heading straight into a bush, and I tried to correct the steering wheel," Michael's dad, Justin, told the website, PerthNow. "When I did that, it tipped over. The last thing I remember was the driver's side hitting the ground."

Michael's dad woke up a few minutes later to find that the truck's cabin had crumpled onto his legs, trapping him between the steering wheel and the dashboard. He was bleeding, and glass was everywhere. The air was ripe with the smell of diesel fuel, which was leaking from the gas tank.

That's when Michael appeared with the tire iron. He hadn't been knocked out like his dad, and when the truck came to a stop, Michael crawled out of the sleeper cabin and got to work. Unfortunately, it was going to take more than a tire iron to bend the metal of the truck enough to let his dad escape.

They needed help. The nearest town—Bonnie Rock, population 63—was about an hour away by

AUSTRALIA
population: 23 million
capital: Canberra

car . . . or about 20 hours of walking on foot. And on that dusty dirt road, it could be hours or even days before another vehicle came along. That's why everyone in Michael's area of remote Western Australia carried a two-way radio! But when Michael looked for the truck's radio, it was gone. When the truck crashed, it had ripped free from its dashboard mount and flown through the windshield. It was sitting in the street, disconnected from the truck battery.

Michael's dad couldn't escape the wreckage without help. The radio was their only hope. Then, Michael noticed that the truck's spare battery had also been thrown from the wreck. He found it in the ditch. The battery weighed about 80 pounds, the weight of a large dog. Michael dragged the battery closer to his dad and then grabbed the radio.

His dad remembered telling Michael to "strip the wires from the radio and put them on the red and blue parts of the battery." Michael did, and the radio crackled with static. Because the big truck battery had way more power than the radio needed, it also shot sparks, burning Michael's hands. As Michael called for help, the whole thing threatened to short-circuit.

Luckily, his mom answered the radio before it blew. The family lived closer to the wreck than an ambulance crew, so Michael's mom organized the neighbors to drive to the rescue. They arrived with the tools needed to pry Michael's dad from the cabin. Forty-five minutes later, an ambulance arrived and Michael's dad was transported to the hospital where he was treated for a concussion, a broken hip, and deep cuts that were filled with pieces of shattered glass.

A member of the ambulance crew called Michael "an outstanding young West Australian whose quick-thinking actions and ability to stay calm in a highly stressful situation helped save his father's life."

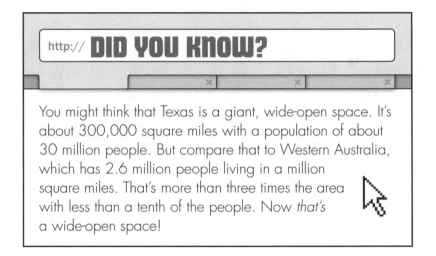

http:// **DID YOU KNOW?**

You might think that Texas is a giant, wide-open space. It's about 300,000 square miles with a population of about 30 million people. But compare that to Western Australia, which has 2.6 million people living in a million square miles. That's more than three times the area with less than a tenth of the people. Now *that's* a wide-open space!

Chapter 2

Creativity

If creativity were just about doing something new, every cat that walked on a piano keyboard would be *very* creative. If we can learn anything from YouTube, it's that keyboard cats are cute, sometimes funny, but never actually *creative*.

That's because being creative isn't just about doing things in a new way. It's about doing things in a *special* new way—a way that has *value*. Do you want to make a creative paper airplane? Just crumple the sheet into a ball! Actually . . . not so much. See, the crumpled ball doesn't have any real value, at least not as a paper airplane. Instead, it takes knowledge of what makes a regular paper airplane so that you know what kind of new idea will help you make a plane that has value.

As you will discover in this section, creativity doesn't just pop into existence like a lightbulb coming on over your head. It's not luck. It's something else . . . something *more*. Maybe by the end of this section, you can figure out what that "something more" is.

Clean Up That Mess!
Jasuel Rivera

When Jasuel Rivera's grandmother saw the pile of cardboard he had collected, she told him to "ese reguero" or "clean up that mess!" But to 13-year-old Jasuel, the cardboard wasn't a mess at all. It was the material he needed to make his machines. Jasuel and his grandmother lived in a neighborhood called El Caimito in the municipality of Yamasa in the Dominican Republic. They couldn't afford fancy Lego kits or technology construction sets, so Jasuel used cardboard, hot glue, wooden craft sticks, toothpicks, and other materials he found in the trash.

Jasuel's cardboard-stick-and-glue contraptions are pretty neat by themselves, but it's the way he uses hydraulics to make them move that makes them super cool. Basically, something that is *hydraulic* uses a liquid to provide force. By pushing fluid through pipes, pistons, and hoses, construction machinery can lift thousands of pounds. In fact, Jasuel got his inspiration from construction sites around his neighborhood.

"I see a parked truck and I try to memorize what it does," he told the Dominican news site, *Cuentas Claras.* "Mechanical things, I record in my mind. But if you send me on an errand, I forget!"

Once you've seen them, it's hard to forget his machines' designs. In one, precisely cut cardboard makes the shape of a bulldozer bucket so perfect that it looks like a miniature of the real machine. Solid, angular arms hold the bucket away from the bulldozer's body. An L-shaped piece attaches the bucket to the

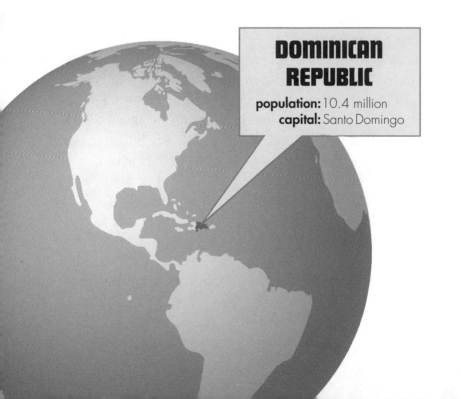

DOMINICAN REPUBLIC

population: 10.4 million
capital: Santo Domingo

arms, pivoting on a round wooden dowel that enables the bucket to tilt up and down. And two hydraulic syringes connected by a hose make the bucket move. With another hydraulic system that raises and lowers the arms, Jasuel uses his cardboard bulldozer to pick up piles of paper scraps that he cut up to look like bricks. He has also built an excavator, a mower, a crane truck, and a dump truck.

For a while, Jasuel wondered if the hydraulic fluid used in real construction equipment would make his machines stronger. This led him to learn about Pascal's principle of transmission of fluid pressure. In the 1600s, French mathematician Blaise Pascal discovered that the less you compress a liquid, the more power it has to push things. If you think about it, it makes sense: If you used your thumb to cap a hose filled with marshmallow paste, the marshmallow would compress instead of pushing against your thumb. A liquid like water doesn't compress as much, so it would push harder. Today, most hydraulic fluids are based on mineral oil, which compresses even less than water.

Jasuel didn't have hydraulic fluid, but his grandmother had drain cleaner, which he thought seemed similar. However, after experimenting, Jasuel found that drain cleaner didn't work much better than water, and it sure smelled bad. He decided to stick with good old H_2O. Sometimes even the best engineer has to learn the hard way!

After *Cuentas Claras* told Jasuel's story, people around the country noticed his resourceful skills and determination. The Dominican Ministry of Education funded a scholarship for Jasuel to attend the Technological Institute of the Americas in Santo Domingo, which will be waiting for Jasuel when he is ready. The Ministry also gave his school, Rosalio de la Rosa, a pair of small programmable robots and chose the school as a test center for a new technology program.

For now, Jasuel will keep experimenting with the materials he finds in the world around him. Cardboard, sticks, glue, and other "trash"? It's all good! Jasuel Rivera knows that creativity isn't about what supplies you have, but *how you use them.*

http:// **DID YOU KNOW?**

All it takes is a quick online search to find pictures of Jasuel Rivera's amazing machines!

Origami Salami
Calista Frederick-Jaskiewicz

Calista Frederick-Jaskiewicz knows the recipe for creativity. First, you have to be deeply curious about lots of things. "Since I learn everywhere, there is no artificial line between life and learning. We learn everywhere, all the time," she wrote in a live chat with the Texas Association for the Gifted and Talented. Calista's curiosity has helped her explore things like acting, art, musical theater, poetry, and piano.

Second, it may seem like creativity springs out of thin air, like a lightbulb popping on over your head, but actually it takes hard work. Even as a full-time high school student who also takes college classes at the Robert Morris University School of Engineering, Mathematics and Science, Calista still makes time to explore her creative hobbies.

Finally, you have to focus all those little snippets of skill and information and hard work into a special activity where a deep creativity can blossom.

In case you didn't guess it from the title, Calista's special skill is origami.

"When I was around six years old, I got an origami kit, and I've been folding ever since!" she says. Origami is trickier than it sounds. You've probably made a paper fortune-teller, or maybe even an origami frog or crane, but Calista's favorite thing to fold is an origami stop motion teabag deer. Just like it sounds,

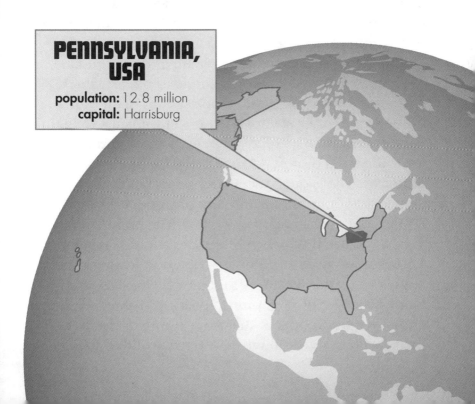

PENNSYLVANIA, USA

population: 12.8 million
capital: Harrisburg

it's a reindeer folded from the paper wrapper around a teabag. The folds are diamonds, trapezoids, and triangles arranged in fractals of high and low creases. The order and angles of these folds are like a multistep math problem in which every step has to be precise in order to finish with the correct answer. Unfold a stop motion teabag deer or any of the other complex origami figures and you unfold a complex world of interlocking geometry.

In Calista's mind, there is no difference between the art of origami and the mathematics of shapes and space that make it possible. That's why, when Calista was 14 years old, it wasn't such a leap for her to combine the two—art and mathematics—in the organization she started called Origami Salami. The club uses the science of paper folding to inspire kids to study science, technology, engineering, art, and mathematics (maybe you've heard of STEAM?).

Today, 20 after-school chapters of Calista's Origami Salami exist in places like Denver, Boston, and New York City, and also in Australia, the Philippines, and Hungary. The groups meet after school to practice classic origami projects and to make up their own.

A piece of origami is like a floating soap bubble: When you see it, you can't help but smile. Calista's organization uses origami to send good feelings and support into the world. For example, after the Sandy Hook school shooting, Calista's groups folded 10,131 cranes for the people of the town. Many of the cranes included handwritten wishes of peace folded inside.

Later, 5,050 of them were displayed at the Carnegie Science Center in Pittsburgh. The organization also teamed up with the Zoological Society of London to raise awareness of the dwindling number of wild elephants. Origami Salami members helped fold 40,000 paper elephants, one for each wild elephant still alive. Chapters have held folding parties to raise money or show support for causes ranging from after-school music programs to a project called "Cranes after the Rains," which sent origami cranes to survivors of Typhoon Haiyan in the Philippines.

Calista knows there are *four* ingredients to creativity. First, she collects influences from all her other activities. Second, she practices for hours every week. Third, she dives deep into the field of origami. And the fourth ingredient: She connects her talent and enthusiasm with the world. She uses her creativity to help other people . . . in creative ways!

http:// **DID YOU KNOW?**

If you're inspired to fold for good, or just to fold for fun, you can start an Origami Salami club, too. Check out origamisalami.com for details.

Creativity Is Inside You
Shubham Banerjee

If you're reading this with your eyes, then chances are you can also go online and read anything you want. Want to know how to build a Popsicle stick catapult? Instructions are just a Google search away. Same goes for inspiration: You can search the Internet for things that make you laugh, cry, think, and look at the world in a different way.

But what if you were blind? When you imagine being blind, you probably think about all the everyday things that might be harder for you to do. It would be harder to get around your house and figure out how to get from class to the lunchroom at school. It might be less fun to go to an art museum or science center or to the zoo. But what about all the information and inspiration you can find through a computer? How important do you think it is to have communication, information, and inspiration at your fingertips?

Shubham Banerjee, a seventh grader from Santa Clara, California, was home one afternoon when the doorbell rang. When he answered the door, no one was there. Instead, he found a flyer hanging from the doorknob. It was a request for donations to help visually impaired people (Shubham himself is sighted). The flyer made him think. *How* do *blind people read?* He asked his parents, and his dad told him to Google it.

Blind people, he learned, can buy a braille display that turns the words on a computer screen into patterns of raised dots. It costs about $3,000. They can buy braille printers, too, that lay down lines of dots. Printers cost anywhere from $1,200 to more than $4,000. Shubham thought this was too much to ask of families who wanted to print readable materials for their blind children. So, he set out to build his own, less expensive braille printer.

Shubham started with a LEGO Mindstorms EV3 kit and about $5 in add-ons from Home Depot. First, he built the base of the printer. Technix pieces make a frame for motorized rubber tires that pull paper off a roll through the printer. Another piece of the base holds the small EV3 computer that is the printer's brain. Finally, he added the highly specialized non-LEGO pieces: a thumbtack and some small metal washers. Shubham uses these pieces to make the print head. As tires pull paper off the spool, the EV3 drives the print head and the thumbtack punches precise holes through the paper in patterns that can be read by a person who knows braille. All together, it costs about $350.

Shubham's dad is a computer engineer at Intel. His dad has also started technology companies. The family lives at the center of technology culture in California. So you might think that while Shubham takes credit for the design of his braille printer, it was his dad and experienced engineers near where they live who actually built it.

But, that's not the case at all.

Shubham's braille printer wasn't designed, built, or promoted by adults. It was born of his mind, hands, experience with LEGOs, and hours and hours of

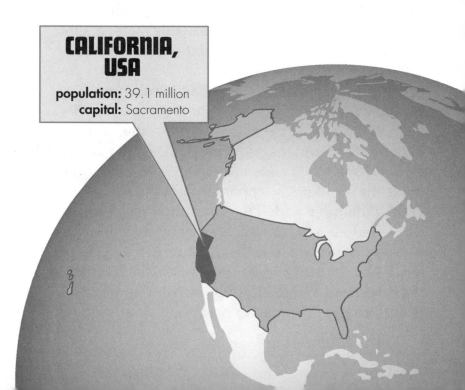

CALIFORNIA, USA

population: 39.1 million
capital: Sacramento

research. Basically, he recognized a problem, looked at the resources he had lying around the house, and used his creativity, his intelligence, and these tools to solve the problem.

Here's another cool thing about true creativity: You won't be creative unless something inside you wants to do it. You can't be creative for a reward. You can't light the spark of creativity if you're forced to do it. Creativity is something that comes from your own desire to invent, learn, work hard, solve problems, imagine, and make something on your empty kitchen table that didn't exist before.

That's what Shubham had. His LEGO printer was born of a need to create what was inside him.

Now he has help from Intel Capital, which invested in his company, Braigo Labs. Braigo hopes to take what Shubham learned from his LEGO braille printer and use it to make lightweight, inexpensive, easy-to-use printers for sightless people around the world. Like many inventions that disrupt the usual way of doing things, Shubham's Braigo printer keeps the one brilliant innovation from the original LEGO design: Instead of costly bubble inks, it uses a pin to punch holes in paper. It's an effective, easy, inexpensive way to do something that used to be difficult and expensive.

Look around. Do you see a problem or something that seems a lot more difficult or more expensive than it should be? From Google's self-driving cars to NASA's hope to send humans to Mars, creative adults around the world are looking at the world through the same lens. When you recognize a problem, ask what makes it a problem. Do some research. Figure out the tools and materials you would need to create a solution. And then look at all that empty space on your kitchen table and *imagine* what you could do to solve this problem.

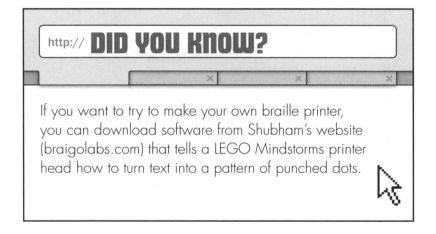

http:// **DID YOU KNOW?**

If you want to try to make your own braille printer, you can download software from Shubham's website (braigolabs.com) that tells a LEGO Mindstorms printer head how to turn text into a pattern of punched dots.

A Monster to Love
Sam and Ben Tollison

Ben draws. Sam sews. Together, the 10-year-old twins from Fort Collins, Colorado, make monsters. But these aren't scary monsters that give you bad dreams. Ben and Sam make cute, odd, creative monsters that look like something Dr. Seuss might draw after eating a rotten hard-boiled egg. One design looks like a sock with tiny ears and an oversized mouth with three rounded teeth. Another is a disturbed teddy bear with a triangle head and off-kilter eyes. Another design looks a little bit like a cyclops bunny with squid arms. Ben and Sam sell these monsters at their website.

Because the boys are fraternal twins, it seemed natural that every monster should have a double, too—almost but not exactly the same. So for every monster that someone orders, the boys draw, cut, stitch, and stuff another one like it. For every monster they mail to families using them as birthday presents and fun little gifts, they send its twin to a children's hospital or children's aid organization.

Sometimes, their customers know where they want the twin to go. Maybe they have it sent to a sick family member, classmate, or friend. Sometimes, people just want the twin monster to bring a smile to someone who needs it. Jennifer Varner works for an organization called Realities for Children, which helps abused and neglected children near where Ben and Sam live. The kids Varner works with have gotten many monsters from the boys.

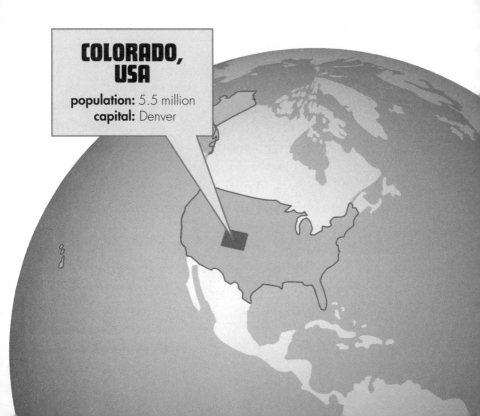

COLORADO, USA

population: 5.5 million
capital: Denver

"Every time they see one of those crazy, little monsters, their eyes light up," Varner said in an interview with the Associated Press. "We tell them the story, that these other children created the monster because they didn't want them to be alone."

The boys also send monsters to the Children's Inn at the National Institutes of Health, and to World Relief, a charity that helps refugee children from war-torn areas of the world who have resettled in the United States.

"Ben can do some pretty crazy monsters," their father, Ray, told the *Denver Post*, "but Sam and I are not the greatest sewers in the world. We keep them simple for now."

See, Ben and Sam aren't professional toy designers. They're two kids with a sketchpad and a sewing machine. And before they started making monsters, they didn't really know how to use the sewing machine!

"I don't think receiving a plush monster is going to change the world, but for a few minutes, it's something that's fun and it's something they can have," says their dad.

Sam and Ben know that with a little creativity and a little follow-through, you can make things happen. These "things" can make the world a better place: Who doesn't like ugly-cute monsters?

Now in the summers, the family tours crafts fairs in their 1971 Volkswagen pop-top camper. If you live near Fort Collins, Colorado, look for Monsters to Love at Maker Faires, craft fairs, art festivals . . . and of course, anywhere a kid could use a special hug from a unique, ugly little monster.

http:// **DID YOU KNOW?**

You can check out Sam and Ben's designs or order a beautiful, ugly little monster of your own at amonstertolove.com.

Mistakes Are Part of the Painting
Amanda LaMunyon

Twelve-year-old Amanda LaMunyon waited nervously in a room next door to the New York City auditorium where she would deliver a speech to the United Nations. At the time, she says, she was obsessed with American Girl dolls, and her mom had promised that if she gave her speech to the crowd, they would go to American Girl Place on Fifth Avenue. The waiting room had an intercom system. All Amanda had to do was push a button and she could deliver her speech from the safety of the private little room!

Four years earlier, Amanda had been diagnosed with Asperger's syndrome. Today, she was speaking to the United Nations as part of World Autism Awareness Day. It would have been terrifying for anybody. It was even harder for Amanda. She grew up in Enid, Oklahoma, nicknamed "The Wheat Capital of the United States," and from the time she was very young, it was obvious that Amanda was different.

"I used to have a reverse fear of heights," she says. "I would go with my mom to the store and look up at the high ceiling and freak out. I would lie down. I would say, 'I feel like I'm going to be sucked up to the ceiling!'"

FAST FACTS

Asperger's syndrome can make it difficult to read social cues, but it often comes with a deep intelligence.

In the school lunchroom, it always seemed like too much was going on. Sometimes, she got so overwhelmed by distractions in class that it felt like the only way to keep from spinning out of control was to get up and leave. So, that's what she did, sometimes just standing up and walking out the door with no explanation. Amanda started going to school for half-days only and coming home at lunch.

"Some people know what to do around other people. And then there's me, staring blankly into space wondering what I should do now. What rules should I follow? Why is it that some things are acceptable in one situation and not acceptable in others? I've had to learn this stuff through trial and error," she says.

Thinking about being in the waiting room before her speech, Amanda says, "It wasn't even just that I was nervous. I was impatient. Things kept happening, and we kept getting delayed. The schedule was off.

Something was wrong. I had a plan in my head about the way it was supposed to work, and it wasn't working that way. And I just wanted to push the button, give my speech, and leave."

In those minutes when her mind started to get away from her, Amanda thought about painting.

She started painting when she was seven. Her first painting was a watermelon. She still has it, but she says it's not very good and so she doesn't like people to see it. But Amanda kept at it and, with lots of practice, her painting improved.

"It helped because it meant I wasn't just weird. I was talented," she says. "Instead of looking at me and wondering what was going on, painting gave people something positive to see when they saw me."

Amanda started painting more and more. Mostly, she painted landscapes, and she loved to paint flowers.

"You don't have to be exact. When you make a mistake, it can become part of the painting. A mistake can make the painting evolve. That way it's more than what you see on the surface. There are layers and it's deeper," she says.

Amanda has learned to see the same thing in herself. The things that make life challenging make her deeper. That's what she thought about in the waiting room at the United Nations. She could understand that the schedule wasn't perfect, but it was okay. She could see that her difference was an essential piece of her talent. It was her job to help the audience see this, too.

Amanda stepped up to the microphone. She told the audience, "When I put a paintbrush in my hands for the first time, I instantly felt my life change. I could finally focus without getting distracted, and my paintings helped me convey everything I had difficulty expressing."

Now, Amanda talks about going out for dinner on Valentine's Day when she was 16. "It was so loud," she says. "There was so much going on. If I had done that at seven, before I started painting, I would have been freaking out. It was still hard for me, but through art, I learned to channel it out."

Amanda also started giving back. She gives prints of her paintings to auctions that raise money

OKLAHOMA, USA
population: 3.9 million
capital: Oklahoma City

for sick kids. She speaks at events raising awareness for autism. And she has won many awards for
her artwork and her charitable work, including the
Prudential Spirit of Community Award and the 2008
Outstanding Individual with Autism Award. Amanda
is in college now, where she is majoring in art and
psychology. One day, she hopes to earn a Ph.D. and
become a psychologist. She wants to work with people
on the autism spectrum.

For now, though, what she really wants to do is
paint.

"When I paint, I feel like I'm one with the paintbrush. I'm able to focus all my energy and all my
thoughts on the painting," she says.

Amanda knows that our perfect imperfections
bring beauty into the world.

Chapter 3

Kindness

A simple act of kindness is bringing a piece of homemade peach pie to your elderly neighbor. But what if your neighbor can't eat sweet treats or is allergic to peaches? True kindness requires looking at the world from another person's perspective. If you were in your neighbor's position, maybe *you* would want peach pie, and you might understand that delivering pie would earn praise from your friends and family. But real kindness looks at the world not with your eyes but with someone else's. In fact, so many acts of kindness are just that: a way to show someone that you understand his or her perspective—you understand the way someone else sees the world.

How good does it feel to know that someone understands, cares, and respects who you are? Beyond money or gifts, it is this feeling of being understood and supported that is at the heart of kindness.

You have the opportunity to help someone feel this feeling. Maybe instead of peach pie, your neighbor would rather have a tomato from your garden. Or if a friend has a problem, maybe you could listen without distraction. Today, practice looking at the world with someone else's eyes. Then, find a way to show that you see what this person sees. That's kindness.

600 Acts of Kindness
Alex McKelvey

How do you honor someone you love who passes away? Unfortunately, Alex McKelvey of Lakewood, Washington, had to ask herself that question when she was only six years old. That year, her grandmother, Linda, died. Alex enlisted her mom, Sarah, to help her perform 60 acts of kindness on March 22, 2014, the day that would have been her grandmother's 60th birthday. These nice things went beyond saying thank you after dinner or helping fold the laundry.

"I try to do acts of kindness at home, but they don't count," Alex told her hometown newspaper, the *News Tribune*. "You have to do them for someone you don't know, or as a surprise for someone you do know, like one of your teachers."

With her mom's support, Alex went on a kindness blitz, offering to pay for coffee or ice cream for people just ahead of them in line, and buying toys for the St.

Jude's Children's Hospital. When they left a big tip
for their waitress at IHOP, Alex took a picture of the
receipt and posted it to Instagram. The waitress found
the picture and wrote, "That was me!!! I didn't even
get a chance to thank them. I'm very grateful to have
been part of this. Thank you so much from me and
my daughter."

March 22, 2014, was a long day, but they made
it— 60 acts of kindness in all! It went so well that Alex
didn't want to stop there. She talked her mom into
helping her complete 600 acts of kindness before what
would have been her grandmother's next birthday in
March 2015.

Off they went. Alex became known as the "napkin
girl" at the Rescue Mission in Tacoma, Washington,

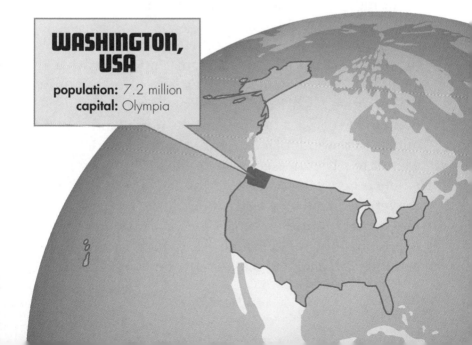

WASHINGTON, USA

population: 7.2 million
capital: Olympia

where it was her job to hand out napkins when she volunteered every week. And she has led an effort to repaint the youth room at the YMCA in her hometown. But most of her acts of kindness don't take many days or hundreds of dollars. Some require only a couple words or a smile.

In March 2015, Alex was closing in on her goal of 600 acts of kindness. She'd spent the year, day in and day out, checking off her list and she wanted to finish strong. So, just like Alex and her mom had started the year of kindness with a day of 60 good deeds, she wanted to cross the finish line with another big day, this time with 61 acts of kindness. Alex knew she would have to get organized, so she made a list and posted it to Instagram with the hashtag #ForLinda, her grandmother's name. Here are some of the things she planned for that day.

Hold the door open for someone, shake someone's hand and thank him, leave a thank-you note with a small treat for the mail carrier, pick up litter and throw it away, give away hugs, give a compliment, deliver homemade cookies to a fire station, leave kindness quotes in random places, return shopping carts, mail a letter to a friend, post positive thoughts on a mirror where others can see, brighten someone's day with flowers, tell someone I love them, leave lucky pennies on the ground for others to find, leave a note in a random book for someone else to find, hand out balloons, tell a joke to make someone laugh, call my grandparents, give someone a high-five and tell her something positive about herself.

Phew! That's a big day! And that's only *part* of the list. The trick is, Alex did more than list these things. She actually did them. All of them and more!

Not many of us will decide to be Alex. Can you imagine doing *half* the things on that list in just one day? Luckily you don't have to. In fact, you don't *have* to do anything on that list. But, today, why not pick one of these small acts of kindness and give it a try? You might find the smiles you create showing up on your own face, too.

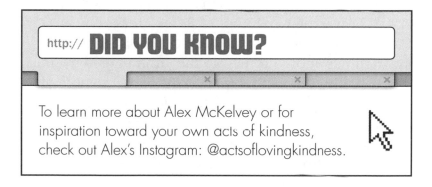

http:// **DID YOU KNOW?**

To learn more about Alex McKelvey or for inspiration toward your own acts of kindness, check out Alex's Instagram: @actsoflovingkindness.

@OsseoNiceThings
Kevin Curwick

You know about cyberbullying. It's when people go online or use their cell phones to text or post mean things about other people. Online, people can say mean things anonymously so they don't get in trouble and they don't have to live with the consequences of the things they say. If you're the target of cyberbullying, you might not even know who your bully is. In 2012, that's what was happening at Osseo Senior High School, in a suburb just northwest of Minneapolis, Minnesota.

"In July, between my junior and senior years, some Twitter accounts were made. Things like 'Osseo Rumors,'" 16-year-old Kevin Curwick said at the time. "Essentially they were anonymous attacks on students at my high school. You could be walking down the hall, and you would look at the people around you . . . even at your best friends, and you don't know who is tweeting these disgusting and awful things about you."

Kevin was quarterback and captain of the football team, captain of the Nordic ski team, president of the National Honor Society, and active in the junior rotary. Everyone knew him, and for the most part, people liked and respected him. So you can imagine that if Kevin had taken a stand against cyberbullying and told his friends—the popular kids at school—to knock it off, they might have listened just because of who he was. After all, Kevin was popular and powerful, and that's how it usually works in high school.

Instead, Kevin decided to fight fire with fire. Or maybe it was more like fighting fire with water.

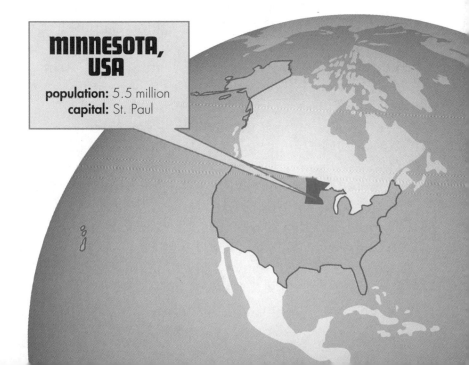

MINNESOTA, USA

population: 5.5 million
capital: St. Paul

What's the opposite of cyberbullying on Twitter? Well, to Kevin, the opposite was cyber *kindness,* in this case anonymous Twitter praise. Kevin started the Twitter account @OsseoNiceThings. And he didn't tell anyone he was behind it. Here are some of the first things he wrote:

"There are too many good people in Osseo to have any one of their reputations ruined."

"Shout out to the incoming sophomores! Help make Osseo what it is #thebest."

"Who has made your experience at Osseo better? Respond and I will retweet for everyone to see."

"Clarke Sanders. If she can't help you feel like a part of Osseo, no one can."

"Only man at Osseo to be known to pull off short shorts. Great runner. Great friend. Quinn Gamble."

"I knew these people and I knew their talents," Kevin says. "And once I started tweeting about them, within a week all those other accounts—the stuff like Osseo Rumors and Osseo Truths—they had all closed." Kevin noticed that everyone was taking part. If @OsseoNiceThings tweeted about a band member, the football team would retweet it. If it was a nice thing about somebody on the girl's golf team, people from the National Honor Society would retweet it.

People outside Osseo started to notice. It started with this tweet: "@OsseoNiceThings Hey. I'm Jay Olstad w/ KARE 11. I have a question for you. Can you email me? Thanks!" Jay was a reporter from a local television station, and when Kevin sat down for an interview that was broadcast on TV, the cat was out of the bag: Osseo Nice Things was no longer anonymous, and everyone learned that Kevin was the person who had started it.

"One thing I stress is that, sure, everybody's crediting me with this idea, but it was anonymous for the first month it ran. The high school took this and ran with it. It didn't need to be me. I absolutely think anybody could have done this. And it could have happened anywhere," Kevin says.

One of the people Kevin connected with through Osseo Nice Things was Dr. Michele Borba, parenting expert for TV shows like *The Today Show* and *The View* and *The New York Times*. Kevin talked with Dr. Borba for a book she was writing about how social media promotes mean and self-degrading comments—we share little snarky things that let us laugh *at* people rather than *with* people.

"But Osseo Nice Things showed how much hunger we had for kindness," Kevin says.

When summer break ended and Kevin and his classmates returned to school, the difference was obvious. "In the cafeteria, there were circle tables that had always been kind of reserved for seniors and jocks and the popular kids, and the surrounding areas were for underclassmen and less popular people. That fall, after Osseo Nice Things, if you walked into the cafeteria, you couldn't see those categories. It was change from social media that went way past social media," Kevin says.

"Whether on Twitter or in person, you can always choose kindness. When you're kind, you build Osseo Nice Things in your life," Kevin says.

How long do you think it takes to start a Twitter account? Maybe 90 seconds if you're a slow typist? Do you wish there were more "nice things" at your school? If you know how to do it (and it's okay with your parents!), why not try to bring a little more kindness to your community?

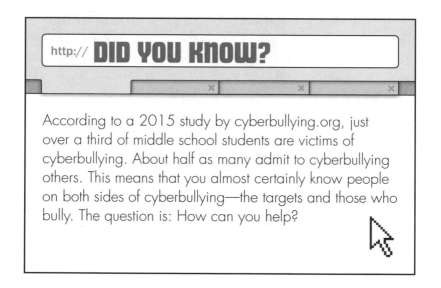

http:// **DID YOU KNOW?**

According to a 2015 study by cyberbullying.org, just over a third of middle school students are victims of cyberbullying. About half as many admit to cyberbullying others. This means that you almost certainly know people on both sides of cyberbullying—the targets and those who bully. The question is: How can you help?

TENNESSEE

Nice Guys Finish Last
Conner Long

For some people, competing in triathlons is about pushing themselves to the limit. For others, it's about winning. For Conner Long, competing in triathlons is just about crossing the finish line. But almost every time he swims, bikes, and runs a race, he finishes last. That's because he tows, pulls, and pushes his younger brother, Cayden, who was born with cerebral palsy.

About one in 500 babies is affected by cerebral palsy, a condition in which parts of a baby's brain don't work. When Cayden was born, the doctor told the family that Cayden would never walk or talk. But Conner Long wasn't about to let his brother be left out.

When Conner was eight and Cayden was six, Conner asked their mom if he could sign up himself and his brother for the Nashville Kids Triathlon near their hometown of White House, Tennessee. The boys' mother, Jenny, was skeptical. In the kids' triathlon, competitors would swim 100 yards, bike three miles, and run half a mile. Even with Conner's help, it seemed impossible. Could the boys finish? Would Cayden enjoy it? But Conner and Cayden started training, and eventually their mother let them enter.

On the day of the race, Conner swam 100 yards, pulling Cayden in a small raft. Cayden wore a life jacket and smiled the whole time. When Conner came out of the water, a coach the family had met online helped lift Cayden from the raft into the bike trailer for the hilly, three-mile ride. Then Conner pushed Cayden in a stroller for the half-mile run.

An average kids' triathlon competitor completes the course in about 19 minutes. It took Conner and Cayden 43 minutes and 10 seconds. They finished last. As they came across the finish line, Conner pumped his fist in the air. Cayden can't speak with words, but his laughter said it all: For the Long boys, finishing last at a kids' triathlon felt like winning the Kona Ironman World Championship.

"What Conner did for Cayden—that choice to do one little race on a weekend—changed them," their mom told *Sports Illustrated*.

The boys continued to compete in more triathlons and fun runs. In the summer, they had a race most weekends. When Conner lined up with Cayden at the start, or after the boys crossed the finish line, people would congratulate the two, telling them how inspiring they were and wanting to have their picture taken with Conner and Cayden.

It was the exact opposite of how Conner saw people treat his brother on most days.

"One thing that makes me really mad is when people say the 'R' word . . . I just tell 'em that it doesn't matter what he looks like on the outside, it's a matter of what's on the inside. He still has feelings and he understands what you say about him," Conner told *Sports Illustrated.*

Through Conner's kindness, Cayden was able to experience not just the worst of what people can be, but also the absolute best. In 2012, *Sports Illustrated Kids* named Conner and Cayden as SportsKids of the Year. At the award ceremony, basketball star LeBron James cried as he congratulated the brothers on their achievements.

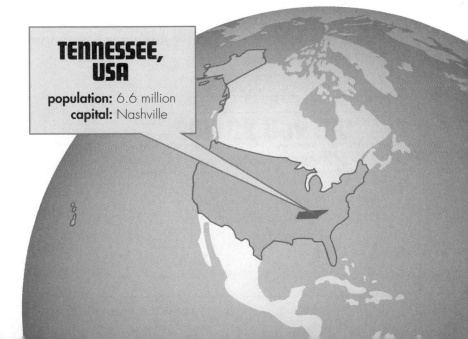

TENNESSEE, USA

population: 6.6 million
capital: Nashville

For some kids, an award like that would be the finish line. But for Conner and Cayden, it was only the start. In 2014, 10-year-old Conner talked the company Miracle Recreation into building a special playground in White House, Tennessee, designed to be accessible to people in wheelchairs and with other challenges. Now, Conner and Cayden can play together. Cayden's favorite part is a wheelchair-accessible swing called the Accelerator that he can sit in while Conner spins him around.

"As soon as we pull up [in the car], Cayden's so excited, and he just loves it a lot," Conner told reporters.

Triathlons, playgrounds, and more, Conner's first goal is to play with his brother. His second goal is to show the world that his brother *can play.*

"Maybe people that didn't care in the past will care in the future," Conner says. If anyone can teach people to care, it's Conner Long.

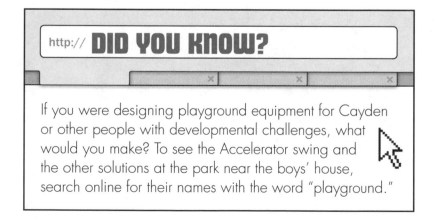

http:// **DID YOU KNOW?**

If you were designing playground equipment for Cayden or other people with developmental challenges, what would you make? To see the Accelerator swing and the other solutions at the park near the boys' house, search online for their names with the word "playground."

People Don't Know and
I Don't Blame Them
Hashmat Suddat

When Hashmat Suddat was young, he lived in a
nice house with his parents, five sisters, and younger
brother in Kabul, the capital city of Afghanistan.
He went to school. One of his older sisters had just
become a teacher.

"Everything was nice before the war," he said.

Then the Taliban came. From 1996 until 2001,
the Taliban ruled Afghanistan. The group ruled
Afghanistan according to the law of Sharia, which was
their interpretation of crime, politics, morality, and
daily life written in the Muslim holy book, the Koran.
The Taliban's form of Sharia thought that women were
meant to be born at home, work at home, and die at
home. Hashmat's older sister had to leave her job as
a teacher. Hashmat's parents spoke out against what
they saw as unfairness during the Taliban rule.

And so his parents were killed.

At 17 years old, Hashmat became an orphan and a refugee. Afghanistan was a bad place for anyone with connections to the anti-Taliban movement, so Hashmat and his siblings decided to leave the country for what they hoped would be a better life in neighboring Pakistan. After a long journey, the family crossed the border into Pakistan to find a life that was nothing like the world they knew. There were no schools, and they had no home. Without parents to protect them and provide for them, Hashmat took whatever jobs he could find, trying to earn enough money to keep his family from having to live in the refugee camp. Hashmat and his family applied for programs that would help them resettle in a country where they could build new lives. Nine hard months later, Hashmat and his siblings were allowed to leave Pakistan to make a home in the United States.

First, the Taliban had changed the family's life in Afghanistan. Then, Hashmat and his siblings had spent almost a year living on what seemed like the face of the moon in Pakistan. And now, they found themselves in an apartment in Virginia.

"If someone had told me that I could look out the window, and as far as my eyes could see, one side of the road would be all white headlights and the other side would be all red lights moving at 60 miles per hour, I would have said they were exaggerating," said Hashmat in an interview with the United Nations High Committee on Refugees (UNHCR).

The timing of their arrival meant the family traded one kind of challenge for another. They arrived in the United States just after the terrorist attacks of September 11, 2001. Hashmat and his family were refugees from Afghanistan, the country that protected Osama bin Laden, the terrorist who planned the September 11 attacks. Hashmat's family has brown skin. They are Muslim. It was not an easy time for Muslim people with brown skin from Afghanistan in the United States, especially for a senior at a new high school.

"Because of September 11, I suffered a lot from the backlash. Students, people in the community thought that Muslims were killers. Terrorists. People didn't

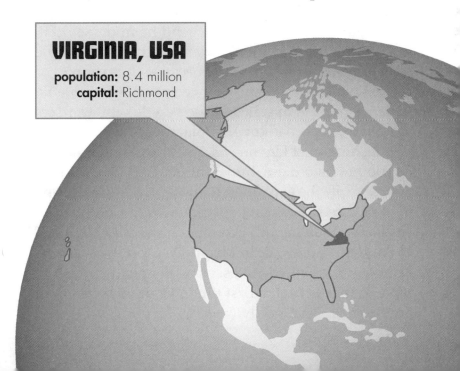

VIRGINIA, USA

population: 8.4 million
capital: Richmond

want to shake hands with me. 'You might have shaken bin Laden's hand.' I explained I was a civilian. Just an ordinary civilian," Hashmat told the UNHCR.

Hashmat's life had already been hard enough. He didn't need kids in Richmond, Virginia, blaming him for terrorist attacks by the same villains who had killed his parents. Hashmat and his family had suffered for years at the hands of the Taliban. And now they were being blamed for the acts of the Taliban as if they supported terrorism.

Still, Hashmat says, "People don't know and I don't blame them."

Hashmat did one of the kindest things that one person can do for another: He *forgave* the people who bullied him for his brown skin, his religion, and the country in which he was born. And he understood that the cure for intolerance is understanding. The people who bullied him were scared because they didn't understand the difference between a refugee from the violence in Afghanistan and the people who were creating the violence in the first place.

Hashmat met fear and racism with kindness, and he tried to help these intolerant people understand. For example, he explained to the UNHCR that people in the United States probably knew more about Osama bin Laden than he did. "You had his picture on the TV. In Afghanistan, we didn't have TV. Or power. When I came to the United States, I saw his picture, who bin Laden was for the first time. We didn't want to be around him. That's why we left," he said.

Someday Hashmat wants to return to Afghanistan to offer the same kindness of forgiveness and education there. "There is less war in Afghanistan now," he says. "But that does not mean peace. Peace means education."

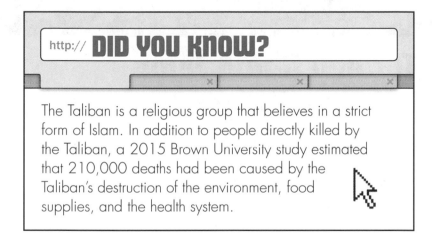

http:// **DID YOU KNOW?**

The Taliban is a religious group that believes in a strict form of Islam. In addition to people directly killed by the Taliban, a 2015 Brown University study estimated that 210,000 deaths had been caused by the Taliban's destruction of the environment, food supplies, and the health system.

Turning Down Fame
Justice Miller

In the small town of Olivet, Michigan, middle school football player Justice Miller was in the right place at the right time to take credit for a heartwarming act of kindness that brought the community together. Justice, the team's star wide receiver, was being interviewed by CBS News about a special play at last night's game.

The team's running back had been sprinting for the goal line with no defenders in sight. Then suddenly, he went down. The coaches and parents thought he'd tripped, but Justice and the rest of the team knew what really happened. They had been planning this moment for two weeks. On the next play, a new running back entered the game—95-pound Keith Orr, usually the team manager, who had a learning disability. Keith's parents had signed him up for football that year hoping he would learn about teamwork. *Hike!* When the next play started, the quarterback handed Keith the ball, and then the team cleared his way into the end zone.

"Nothing can really explain getting a touchdown when you've never had one before," Justice told CBS News.

Keith was an instant celebrity. And the boys on the Olivet Middle School football team had the opportunity to be celebrities, too. Someone just needed to step forward and take credit. But when CBS News asked Justice for an interview, he wrote back, "I think you should really be interviewing our running back. He is the one who took the knee and really made it possible." In other words, wide receiver Justice chose to *take a pass* on the spotlight. He chose to give up the chance to be famous and turn down the opportunity for the entire country to think that he had been the hero behind this beautiful, heartfelt, kind play on the football field.

Scoring a touchdown with his team changed Keith Orr's life. After the game, his coach told the local TV station, "Now the other players eat lunch with him. Now they talk to him in the halls. Keith has discovered there are things he can accomplish he didn't know he was capable of. His mom is now more at ease, knowing that he has friends to last him through high school."

This kindness changed Keith Orr, and it changed Justice Miller, too. Instead of taking credit for the famous play, Justice humbly admits, "I kind of went from being somebody that mostly cared about myself and my friends to caring about everyone and trying to make everyone's day."

Justice's first kindness was being involved in Keith's touchdown, even if it was only by keeping the plan secret and then helping to block for Keith's run into the end zone. But his *true* kindness was and continues to be letting the moment be about Keith and not about himself.

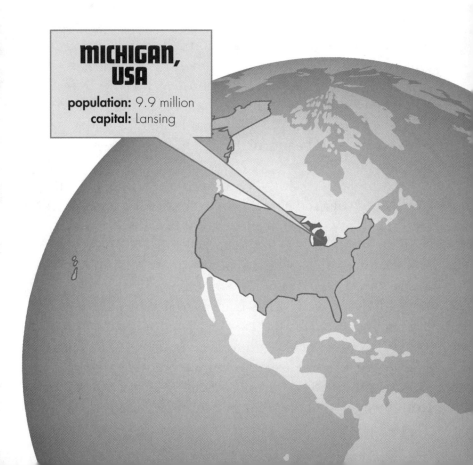

MICHIGAN, USA

population: 9.9 million
capital: Lansing

http:// **DID YOU KNOW?**

You can see the CBS News interview with Justice Miller, Keith Orr, and other members of the Olivet Middle School football team by searching "CBS News touching touchdown."

Chapter 4
Persistence and Grit

You've probably heard the saying, "No person is an island." But wouldn't it be nice if you were! You could sit in the sand under your little palm tree drinking coconut juice while watching the sun set across the ocean! Really, take a second to imagine yourself as an island. Everything that you are makes up your slice of sand—all your intelligence, creativity, and talent go into shaping your island. Maybe you have an island of awesomeness. Maybe your island should be called Awesome Island, the Awesome Island of Total Awesomeness!

Unfortunately, it doesn't matter how awesome you are if you don't *do* anything with it. What good is your natural talent if it stays trapped on an island? Getting from the island of your awesomeness to the mainland of your goals requires a bridge. And that bridge is built from persistence and grit.

No matter how smart you are, how athletic, how well-liked or good-looking, not everything in life will be easy. Some things you try won't work out. Sometimes you will fail. At that point, only the choice to keep trying can lead to meaningful results in the real world. Every time something is hard or doesn't go as planned, you have the opportunity to put another brick in the bridge leading from your island of talent toward your goals.

Of course, the other option is to sit marooned on your island of potential. You might even know somebody like that: all the natural talent in the world but without the persistence to turn talent into results. Maybe you've even felt like that sometimes? Hey, no judging and especially no self-judging! Persistence in the face of the smack-down is terribly, awfully hard.

Next time something is hard or you fail, recognize that you have a choice. You have the choice to do the easy thing, sitting on your island of potential sipping coconut juice, or you can do the hard thing and try again, laying another brick in the bridge of persistence and grit that leads to your goals.

Bubble Ball
Robert Nay

If you watched the eight-hour version of Nyan Cat, your brain would leak out your ears, and you would have to squeegee it into a zipper storage bag and save it in the freezer until future neuroscientists could find a way to reinject it into your skull. The same is true of those simple, addictive apps that you sneak to your locker to play for 30 seconds between classes.

But instead of rotting your brain, what if apps could *build* your brain? Sure, some apps are *meant* to build your brain. But are you really going to play them instead of Angry Birds? At 14 years old, Robert Nay learned the secret. Instead of *playing* mindless apps, Robert decided to *build* them.

Unfortunately, like many kids, Robert knew how to tap on a screen to make a heroic bird destroy an evil pig, but sitting down at a computer and design-ing the cartoons and mechanics that make the game seemed like a powerful and secret magic. Maybe it seems that way to you, too. What would you do if you wanted to learn how to take an idea in your head and create a game that people could download? Robert Nay decided to go to the public library. Even with a world of information at your fingertips, sometimes it takes hunkering down at the library after school to get things done. At the library, Robert wasn't distracted by TV and his brother or sister couldn't annoy him.

Every day for months, Robert Nay spent hours at the public library in his hometown of Spanish Fork, Utah. It's a beautiful building that looks like a cathedral in the small town sandwiched between Utah Lake and Spanish Fork Peak. But Robert Nay wasn't there for the view. He stuck his nose in the library computers and learned to code.

He experimented with the programming platform called "Objective C," but it was too complex. He tried another platform called "GameSalad," but it was too simple. Finally, he tried a game platform called "Corona," and this time, the porridge was juuuust right.

UTAH, USA
population: 3 million
capital: Salt Lake City

In its first two weeks, his app Bubble Ball was downloaded 2 million times. It was the first app to knock Angry Birds from its #1 free game spot in the Apple app store. The game looks simple: You guide a ball through a little physics world to a flag. The first level is so easy, just drag and drop a triangle underneath the ball so that when you click *start* the ball falls onto the triangle, rolls down, and rolls over to the flag. There's a burst of success music, and then it's onto the next level! Drag and drop a metal plank to keep the bubble ball from falling through a hole. Wood blocks obey gravity and metal blocks do not. Watch for springs, teleports, and more!

The graphics are basic. The sound is a little hard on the ears. But the concept is genius. And due to the hundreds of hours Robert Nay spent at the library, the game actually works! It's easy to get hooked on Bubble Ball. Do you think, like Robert Nay, you could get hooked on *making* games like Bubble Ball?

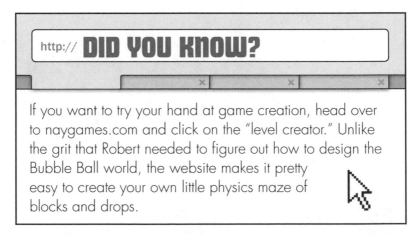

http:// **DID YOU KNOW?**

If you want to try your hand at game creation, head over to naygames.com and click on the "level creator." Unlike the grit that Robert needed to figure out how to design the Bubble Ball world, the website makes it pretty easy to create your own little physics maze of blocks and drops.

Drab to Fab
Christopher Cruz

Cafeteria food sometimes gets a bad rap. Sure, it can be a little gray, a little soggy, and a little squishy, and it might be made from mystery ingredients like ground-up rubber from discarded shoe soles. But if you can look past little things like that, it's pretty delicious . . . if you hold your nose.

Eleven-year-old Christopher Cruz and his friends at New York's PS 123 in Brooklyn, New York, decided that gray food plus their gray basement cafeteria was one too many grays. There wasn't much they could do about the food, so they decided to work on the cafeteria. Instead of gray, what about yellow with a bright green stripe?

First, they needed permission from their principal, so Christopher and his friends wrote her letters. "Every day you wear nice clothes and you look beautiful with different hairstyles," starts a letter by Daisy

Robles, and finishes with, "I hope you give us permission to paint the lunchroom!"

And—what do you know!—the principal, Veronica Greene, gave them permission to paint the cafeteria if they could get the paint and supplies for free and find adult volunteers to help them.

It was a tough task. One gallon of the kind of paint they needed cost about $50, and they were going to need several gallons, plus rollers, brushes, tape, and tarps, and all the other supplies you need to do a professional-looking paint job.

Just like they had written letters to their principal, Christopher Cruz and the other students at PS 123 started writing letters to home improvement stores. They asked for donations and help. But unlike the

NEW YORK, USA

population: 19.8 million
capital: Albany

letters they wrote to their principal, most of the letters they wrote to businesses resulted in a big *No*. It turns out it was easier to get permission than it was to get money and volunteers!

They kept writing. Summer break came, but when the school doors opened in the fall, they were right back to writing letters. When one letter was returned with a *no*, another one went into the mailbox. Eventually, they talked the paint company Benjamin Moore, which started in Brooklyn, into donating paint—"Sunny Yellow" to cover up the gray and bright green "Springtime" for the strip of molding that ran around the wall at about eye level. They got a few more colors, too, like a darker green for some of the pillars and a nice deep red to frame the drinking fountains. Volunteers came from the charity Publicolor. As a result of their letters, Yellow Pages decided to donate $10,000 to cover the other supplies they would need.

Now, the only problem was when to get the paint on the walls. They couldn't use school time for it. And the lunchroom was in use after school. The only time available to Christopher and his growing team was on Saturdays. So every morning for five Saturdays in the fall of 2013, the kids met at the school with their volunteers to paint. With rollers and brushes, they started to turn the dark and dingy lunchroom that made them frown into a bright and colorful space that made everyone smile.

The kids aren't professional painters, and in the photos that go with an article by the *New York Daily*

News, it's hard to tell what got more paint, the students or the walls! Finally, just before winter break in December 2013, the project was finished. It had been almost a year since the students wrote their first letters to their principal! Instead of a wet sock, the lunchroom looked like limes and lemons. Their persistence paid off, and instead of drab, it was *fab*!

Now maybe they can do something about the food?

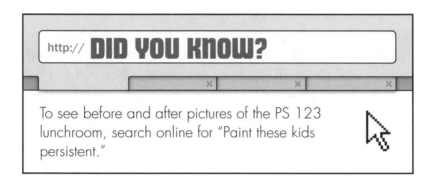

http:// **DID YOU KNOW?**

To see before and after pictures of the PS 123 lunchroom, search online for "Paint these kids persistent."

A Persistent Hunch
Danny DiPietro

On a January night in 2014 that was well below freezing, 10-year-old Danny DiPietro and his dad were driving home from a hockey game. When they pulled into their neighborhood, Danny thought he saw something out of the corner of his eye. Down the block from where he lived, a garage door was up and something inside was moving. Was that a dog in the garage? Danny thought it looked too big to be a dog, but their car passed the garage too quickly to tell. As they pulled into their driveway, Danny's sixth sense kept telling him that something wasn't right.

He asked his mom to go check it out. Now, if you've ever been to Danny's hometown of Howell, Michigan, about an hour northwest of Detroit, then you know it can get downright cold in the winter. And this wasn't just regular winter cold, it was *record-breaking* winter cold. The temperature was below zero and with wind chill, it was −30 degrees Fahrenheit in some places. It wasn't the most pleasant time for a nighttime stroll. Danny's mom told him that he must be imagining things and to forget about it.

Danny said he was worried that a dog might have been left in the garage. His mom said that no one would leave a dog out in such cold weather.

"He wouldn't give up," his mom told the website, Today.com. "Thankfully, he was persistent."

Now *there's* a word that can mean many things. "Persistence" can mean sticking with something when it's hard or after you fail. And it can also mean holding

MICHIGAN, USA

population: 9.9 million
capital: Lansing

true to what you know is right even when other people see things differently.

In an interview with the local TV station, Danny's mom said, "So he walked out of the room and came back and he said, 'No, can we just go up there?'" Danny kept insisting that something wasn't right until his mom finally agreed to check it out.

What his mom found was not a dog. When Danny's mom reached the open garage, she found an elderly neighbor on the ground, barefoot, waving her hands for help. The 80-year-old neighbor had slipped on ice that had fallen off her car. She had tried to scoot herself closer to the door of the garage where she thought people might see her. Unfortunately, she had also scooted herself right into the force of the wind and had lost her shoes and gloves along the way. Danny's mom ran for help! While Danny's dad returned with a blanket, his mom called 911.

Rescuers arrived and rushed the woman to a nearby hospital where she was treated for frostbite and hypothermia. Doctors said the neighbor wouldn't have survived another hour in the freezing cold.

The elderly neighbor's daughter met with Danny to say thank you. The daughter said about her mother, "She is very emotional when she talks about Danny and she says, 'That little boy saved my life. Just thank goodness for that little boy. Thank goodness for his hunch and his persistence.' And she knows as well as everybody else that she's alive because of him."

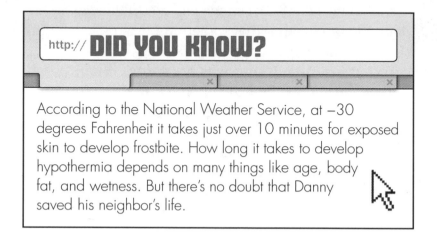

http:// **DID YOU KNOW?**

According to the National Weather Service, at –30 degrees Fahrenheit it takes just over 10 minutes for exposed skin to develop frostbite. How long it takes to develop hypothermia depends on many things like age, body fat, and wetness. But there's no doubt that Danny saved his neighbor's life.

NEW HAMPSHIRE

Practice Makes Perfect
Mikaela Shiffrin

Vail, Colorado, has 33 ski lifts, servicing 193 trails. You can ski 3,450 vertical feet from the top to the bottom. Vail has a reputation for excellent snow, posh hotels, and one of the best youth ski teams in the country. Basically, it is one of the most awesome places you could possibly imagine to ski. It is also where Mikaela Shiffrin was born. As you might expect, Vail is the perfect place for a future ski champion to grow up, right?

But when Mikaela was eight years old, her family moved from Vail to a small town in New Hampshire, near the ski area of Storrs Hill. Storrs Hill has exactly one ski lift. It's only 300 vertical feet from top to bottom. On the way down, you can take the main trail, the back trail, or the terrain park. It has a reputation for being icy. Sometimes it rains. Basically, it's *not* the most awesome place you could possibly imagine to ski. In fact it's pretty dismal, especially compared with

Vail. But Mikaela loved to ski. And even more than that, she loved to *race.*

While youth skiers in Vail were having fun on endless trails of powder, Mikaela Shiffrin was running endless laps at Storrs Hill. While kids on the Vail ski team spent weekends waiting their turn to get only two or three runs at races in the beautiful Colorado mountains, Mikaela was—you guessed it!—still running endless laps in the ice and slush at Storrs Hill.

But when you take away the terrain of a big mountain, the lift lines, and the distractions of moguls, chutes, bowls, and tree skiing, you're left with the bare-bones essence of what it means to ski: your skis on the snow and your body sliding downhill. There was no challenge in getting down the trails at Storrs Hill; the only challenge was getting down *perfectly.*

Run after run after run, that's what Mikaela Shiffrin learned to do. She worked to keep her upper body quiet while learning to put her skis on edge and use her wrist guards to punch down the plastic pole gates that marked the practice course. When racers ski the

FAST FACTS

In skiing, "moguls" are the round bumps that make a slope look like a giant sheet of bubble wrap. A "chute" is a ribbon of snow between things you would rather not hit. And a "bowl" is a wide-open slope that starts steep at the top and flattens out at the bottom, like the shape of a playground slide.

slalom course, you might assume the music in their head must be heavy metal. It looks like every turn they make is hard work, like lifting a wheelbarrow full of rocks that could tip over at any second. But, to help her get psyched, Mikaela listened to classical music by an Italian pianist named Ludovico Einaudi. You can see the influence in her turns, which look precise, smart, and almost effortless.

After thousands of hours of practice and persistence, sometimes at night, often as the only skier on the hill, Mikaela Shiffrin finally started entering races. And once she started racing, she started winning. She won pretty much every youth competition in the United States. At age 14, she started winning world junior competitions, and at age 16, she stood on her first adult World Cup podium.

In January 2014, Mikaela was at a race in Bormio, Italy. It was snowing at the top of the racecourse . . . and raining at the bottom. In between was a mix of sleet and wind, making the course a sloppy mess. With the slush flying up and sticking to their goggles, by the bottom of the course, the racers could barely see where they were going. At the finish line, spectators held umbrellas. Most of the racers were grumbling about the terrible conditions. What did Mikaela think?

"The weather reminds me of Vermont, the Northeast Kingdom," she said. "I got out here this morning, and I was like, 'Yes! Here we go. I'm going to be soaking wet.' You might as well embrace it!" she told skiracing.com.

Skiing Storrs Hill can be brutal and cold and icy and wet. And persevering through these conditions made Mikaela able to bring her A-game to races that were brutal and cold and icy and wet. Just before the last slope at the race in Bormio, Mikaela was only 0.01 seconds ahead of the second place time. But in the rain on the steep final hill, Mikaela dug into the slush and turned on the afterburners! She won the race by 0.13 seconds—a huge margin in ski racing—beating competitors from Sweden, Switzerland, Slovenia, and Germany.

NEW HAMPSHIRE, USA

population: 1.3 million
capital: Concord

In February 2014, at 18 years old, Mikaela won the gold medal in slalom skiing at the Olympic Games in Sochi, Russia. Since then, Mikaela's life hasn't been easy. In 2015, she injured her knee during a training run in Sweden. At first, she thought she would take a vacation someplace warm and skip the ski season. "But the truth is I love ski racing, and it's my job," she told ESPN.

Back home in the weeks after her injury, Mikaela got right back to work, spending long hours perfecting her recovery the same way she perfected her turns all those years ago at Storrs Hill. For Mikaela, persistence isn't something that she used as a kid and then left behind as a professional. Her childhood persistence has become part of who she is as a person.

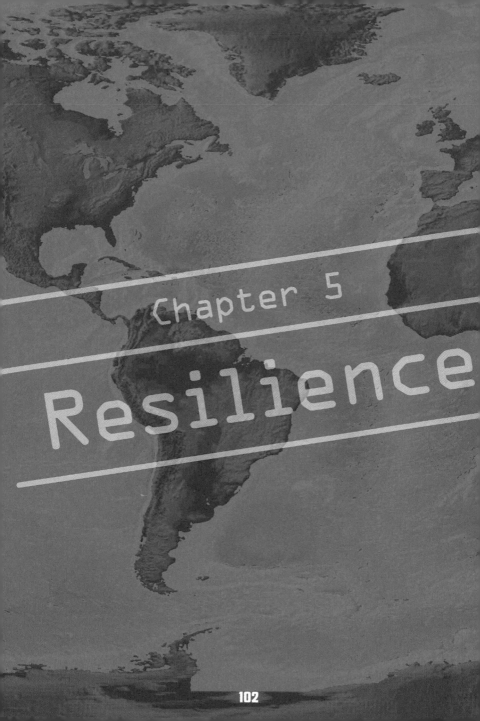

Chapter 5

Resilience

Hey, didn't we just read stories in the last section about people who kept trying when things were hard? Yeah, but there's a huge difference between persistence and resilience: Persistence helps you reach the goals you choose, and resilience is how you deal with the challenges that choose you. If life were fair, we could all be persistent. But here's a news flash: Life isn't fair. Sometimes life requires resilience—the ability to spring back into shape after taking a dent.

But the stories in this section are about more than survival. These young people show that life's challenges can also be opportunities. Sometimes people who spring back into shape take on new shapes they never would or could have imagined before they were challenged. If you are forced to be resilient, you may never be the same as you would have been without the challenge. But maybe with resiliency, you grow into something *more*.

Big Mussels of Science
Samantha Garvey

Samantha Garvey spends a lot of time working on her mussels. In 2012, the 17-year-old Long Island high school senior was worried that crabs were going to eat them. But before you start picturing spider crabs munching on poor Samantha's biceps, take another look at the spelling. It's not "muscles" but "mussels," as in the species *Geukensia demissa,* a shellfish native to the east coast that is being decimated by the Asian shore crab.

Who would win this epic sea life battle of crab versus clam?

At the urging of one of her teachers, Samantha had been working as a research assistant in the laboratory of an ecology professor at nearby Stony Brook University. Samantha's research showed that mussels had a natural defense against the eight-legged invaders. Basically, when she grew mussels in tanks with and without the scent of crabs, the mussels that thought they were in danger of being munched on grew thicker shells. She submitted her findings to the Intel Science Talent Search and learned just after the winter holiday in 2012 that she had been named a semifinalist in the prestigious competition.

At that point, she had been homeless for almost two weeks.

Samantha's family had never been rich. Her parents were immigrants from El Salvador. With her mother working as a nurse and her dad working as a cab driver, they made just enough to afford an apartment in the Brentwood neighborhood of Long Island, New York . . . a place where, if you were to do an Internet search for it, the first results might be of eyewitness crime reports from the local TV station, mug shots of young men, and pictures of a burning train.

During the school year, Samantha worked about 12 hours every week in professor Dianna Padilla's marine ecology laboratory. During summers, Samantha spent almost all day, every day studying mussels and helping with other lab work. "Samantha's level of dedication was incredible," Padilla says.

After taking mussel samples from a marsh called Flax Pond, Samantha grew some of them in tanks with the smell of Asian shore crabs and some in tanks without this smell. Every day, she carefully measured the mussels' growth. Eventually, she was able to show that mussels grown in tanks with crab scent grew more slowly but had thicker shells than mussels grown without the predator scent. This finding is super cool: Mussels could adapt their growth to the needs of their environment. If they thought there were crabs around, the mussels grew thick shells as protection. Without crabs, the mussels converted the energy it would take to grow thick shells into energy to grow quickly to adult size.

With her hard work leading to a clear, important finding, and with the results sent off to the Intel Science Talent Search, Samantha seemed right on track to be a promising young scientist.

But then Samantha's family was in a car accident and injuries forced her mom to quit her job. On December 31, 2011, the family was evicted from their apartment. Samantha, her siblings, and her parents were forced to move into a shelter.

"It's not bad. It's a nice place," Samantha said in an interview with *The New York Times*.

As the eldest of three children, Samantha applied for jobs to help the family. While she was searching for work, she kept working on her science project, even while living in the shelter. A few weeks later, Samantha learned she had been selected as an Intel semifinalist.

It didn't take long for word of Samantha's story to get out. She went on *The Ellen Degeneres Show* to tell her story and earned a $50,000 college scholarship. She attended the 2012 State of the Union Address in Washington, D.C., at the invitation of her congressman, Steve Israel. Most importantly, Suffolk County found a place for her family to live in subsidized housing.

When *The New York Times* asked Samantha what she would be doing if she hadn't chosen to study mussels, she said, "Probably flunking out of school, honestly."

Samantha didn't flunk out. After graduating high school, she started college at Bowdoin in Maine, where she is the "EcoRep" for Burnett House, one of the college's cottage-style dormitories. She's also a student manager at one of the college cafeterias. Sorry to say, she's given up studying mussels. Now Samantha is studying sea stars, watching them for hours and hours to explore how they move.

NEW YORK, USA

population: 19.8 million
capital: Albany

"Understanding eco-processes and how things work, and the place that we live on, even other places as well, I love it," Samantha told the local paper.

It takes resilience to stick with a research project for hundreds of hours to get results. It takes even more resilience when you live in a homeless shelter. Samantha knows what it's like to struggle. And now she also knows what it's like to succeed.

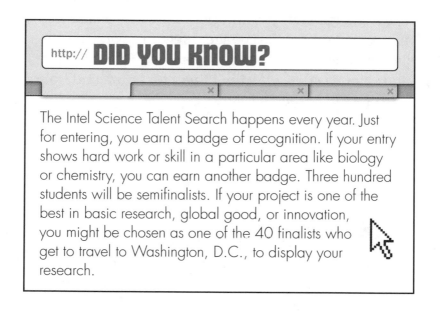

http:// **DID YOU KNOW?**

The Intel Science Talent Search happens every year. Just for entering, you earn a badge of recognition. If your entry shows hard work or skill in a particular area like biology or chemistry, you can earn another badge. Three hundred students will be semifinalists. If your project is one of the best in basic research, global good, or innovation, you might be chosen as one of the 40 finalists who get to travel to Washington, D.C., to display your research.

Ya Sama!
Tatyana McFadden

Tatyana McFadden spent the first six years of her life in a Russian orphanage. She was born with spina bifida, a hole in her spinal column that left her paralyzed from the waist down. The orphanage was too poor to buy her a wheelchair, so she walked on her hands everywhere she went. Try it sometime. How far can you get before your arms get tired?

Over 350,000 children live in Russian orphanages and the odds of being adopted are against them. Most of them leave the orphanages only after they turn 18 and are pushed from the system. Children with a disability are especially unlikely to be adopted.

In 1994, when Tatyana was six, her orphanage received a special visit from the Commissioner for Disabilities for the U.S. Department of Health, Deborah McFadden. Deborah felt an instant connection with little Tatyana and she decided to adopt the small girl who couldn't use her legs.

Deborah did everything she could to help make Tatyana's transition to the United States easier, including getting her a wheelchair. But sometimes Tatyana didn't want assistance. Deborah remembers trying to help Tatyana with mobility or, really, anything, and Tatyana would say, *"Ya sama, ya sama!"* The Russian phrase means, "I can do it myself!" Even though Tatyana had health problems, she also had strong arms from six years of pulling herself around the orphanage.

Not long after arriving in the United States, Tatyana started playing sports in her wheelchair— basketball, ice hockey, and more. She was good at them all, but it was track that stuck.

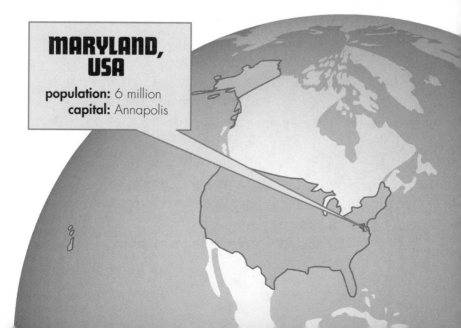

MARYLAND, USA

population: 6 million
capital: Annapolis

At 15 years old, she was the youngest person on Team USA's track squad at the 2004 Paralympics in Athens, Greece, where she won silver and bronze medals. But when she got home to Atholton High School in Columbia, Maryland, she wasn't allowed to race with the school track team. Instead, she had to race in a special wheelchair event. Usually, she was the only athlete. After the able-bodied race finished, Tatyana would make a couple laps around the track by herself and notch a win.

Tatyana didn't think it was fair that she had to race alone. In 2005, Tatyana showed another kind of resilience when she sued the school district for the right to race alongside able-bodied runners. This created a lot of controversy. The school district argued that wheelchair athletes go faster than able-bodied athletes over long distances. The district was also concerned that wheelchair athletes could collide with other racers on the track. Was it fair for Tatyana to race with her classmates? Was it safe?

After much discussion, U.S. District Court Judge Andre Davis ruled in Tatyana's favor, saying, "She's not suing for blue ribbons, gold ribbons, or money—she just wants to be out there when everyone else is out there."

The lawsuit led to the right for all students with physical challenges across the United States to compete in school athletics. The determination and resilience of a girl raised in a Russian orphanage changed the way kids in the United States play sports.

Tatyana has gone on to make history in her sports. In 2013, she became the first person—with or without a health challenge—to win four of the world's major marathons in one year, with wins in Boston, London, Chicago, and New York. Then, she took silver in a cross-country skiing event at the 2014 Sochi Paralympic Games after less than a year of training in the sport. She also played for her college wheelchair basketball team at the University of Illinois!

"If you want it bad enough, you must try. And if you miss the first time, you must try again," Tatyana writes. "Don't let others tell you that your dreams are too big or your ambitions impractical."

http:// **DID YOU KNOW?**

At tatyanamcfadden.com, you can learn about Tatyana's life and also find inspiring stories and sports resources, whether you race in a wheelchair or not.

My Name, My Story
Amit Dodani

Try saying the word *good*. Do you feel the back of your tongue making the "g" sound? Now imagine your tongue doesn't want to make that sound. In fact, imagine your tongue refuses to make *any* back-of-the-tongue sounds like "g" or "k" or "x" or "q." Instead of *good*, it would sound like *dood*. Instead of *car*, it would sound like *tar*. And you would sound . . . well, you would sound like Amit Dodani, who has a speech impediment. Despite speech lessons, he couldn't force the back of his tongue to make the sounds his brain wanted.

Amit's parents own a technology company in San Jose, California. Part of being a business owner is speaking to groups of employees, customers, and other businesses. At one of their company meetings, Amit's parents invited him to speak for a couple minutes, too. His parents hoped that speaking in front of people would give Amit the opportunity to accept his unique way of speaking—to stand proud in front of a crowd despite the difference in the way he pronounced words.

Amit spent hours writing his three-minute speech. He spent many more hours memorizing it and practicing in front of a mirror. Finally, the day of the speech arrived. But despite all his practice, the second Amit opened his mouth everything went wrong. For Amit, it seemed like time slowed down just so he could watch himself acting like an idiot in slow motion. Amit could hear himself stumbling over the words but he couldn't do anything to stop it. Being nervous only made things worse. His whole body started shaking, and in the middle of his speech, Amit felt tears running down his cheeks. When he finally finished, Amit jumped from the stage and ran from the room.

The next year, Amit's aunts and uncles planned a surprise party in a hotel ballroom for Amit's parents. They asked Amit to say a couple words to the guests. Amit reluctantly agreed—he couldn't very well say no. But when he stood on stage looking out at nearly a hundred people in the audience, he knew the words weren't going to come out right. With everyone watching, he bolted from the stage.

"They were shocked," Amit says, "I mean, my parents were public speakers. Everyone thought it would be natural for me to be the same, but of course, it wasn't."

Amit decided this was the end of his public speaking career. He was teased at school, and despite being an excellent student, he even stopped raising his hand in class. He wanted to sink into the background of school and life so he wouldn't have to embarrass himself by opening his mouth. He started to feel like his failure to speak like everyone else meant that he was a failure altogether. He was different. He was damaged. His speech impediment made it impossible for him to be the person everyone expected him to be. More than anything, he felt like he had disappointed his parents.

Toward the end of seventh grade, Amit's teacher told the class about tryouts for the eighth grade mock trial team. His middle school was known for the excellence of this team—sometimes their mock trial team even made it all the way to the state championships!

CALIFORNIA, USA

population: 39.1 million
capital: Sacramento

Here's how mock trial works: At the beginning of the school year, teams get packets of information describing a crime, evidence, and all the laws that relate to the case. As an after-school club, teams prepare to argue both sides of the case, with some students trying to prove that a person accused of the made-up crime is guilty and others trying to prove the person is innocent. Team members practice being witnesses, and a few students are assigned the roles of attorneys.

"It was kind of crazy—the idea of a kid who has a speech impediment trying out for an activity based on speech," Amit told the *Ventura Boulevard* magazine. But Amit realized he had a choice: If he didn't try out for the team, he would be admitting that the way he talked made him unable to do things that other students could do. But if he tried out . . . who knew? At least he would still be trying.

Not only did Amit try out, he made the team!

During his eighth-grade year, Amit worked with the two mock trial coaches to slow down, imagine the shapes of words, and stay focused inside his own head instead of letting the crowd, the pretend jury, or the coaches make him nervous. Just before winter break, the coaches had to assign roles—who would be witnesses and who would get the parts of the two attorneys?

When he tried out for the role of defense attorney, Amit remembers "staring right into the piercing eyes of my coach." Despite his hard work, he felt just like he had in fifth grade when he stood in front of his parents' business partners and just like he had in sixth grade while trying to speak at the family gathering. "I was totally shaken up to the point where my coach asked me if I was okay afterward," he says.

One of the coaches was skeptical—Amit's pronunciation was far from perfect and it was obvious he was nervous. But the other coach saw something in Amit. Maybe it was his courage. Maybe the second coach could see how much he wanted it.

"Long story short, I got the part. I don't know how, but I did," Amit says.

Much later, after his team had won the state mock trial competition at the Los Angeles courthouse and Amit had received a perfect score in every round, he sat on the school's small activity bus talking with the coach who had doubted him. "Amit," his coach admitted, "the first time you delivered that closing argument, I *never* thought you would come this far."

But for Amit, "this far" was only the start. That year, his team took fifth at the national mock trial competition, and Amit earned the award for the 11th best speaker in the country. Not bad for a guy who couldn't say the letter "g"!

After the competition, Amit realized that his real challenge had never been his speech impediment. His challenge was overcoming the way his impediment made him feel about himself. He also realized it was just one of many things that can make kids want to stop trying and give up.

So Amit started the organization My Name, My Story (MNMS) as a place where kids can come together to feel proud of the differences that make us all unique. Today, 14 schools have MNMS clubs with over 100 leaders, all working to inspire empathy in their communities.

"To this day, I still get the occasional 'What did you just say?' But now, all that doesn't matter," Amit says. "All the frustration, all the tears, all the jokes that used to happen, they all were part of the journey."

Amit knows that the way he speaks won't hold him back from the things he could become. He says that, "Anybody who is willing to keep trying, even when things get hard or when things don't work, can turn their biggest weakness into their greatest strength."

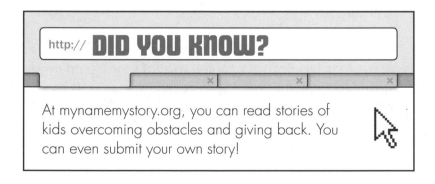

http:// **DID YOU KNOW?**

At mynamemystory.org, you can read stories of kids overcoming obstacles and giving back. You can even submit your own story!

Victor Not Victim
James Williams

This is a story about child abuse. It shouldn't have to be written and you shouldn't have to read it. Sometimes life is terribly unfair, but as you will see, this is also a story of hope and resiliency.

When James Williams was one year old, he was riding in the backseat of his father's car. His father had been drinking. Again. And when his dad was pulled over by the police, James was placed in a foster care group home.

> If this story is upsetting to you, find someone you trust to talk with about it.

When James was five, a family adopted him, and for a couple years everything went well. "Then everything seemed to spiral downward when they started to hit me," he writes. When he was 12, his adoptive family sent James to live with his biological grandmother. Unfortunately, his dad was living there as well. "He didn't say a word to me. He just came in drunk. I ran away," says James.

Over the next few years, James moved through a handful of group and foster homes. Some situations were positive. Some were not. At one of these homes, his foster father "made derogatory remarks about other races," James remembers. And one night, after seeing James hanging out with an African-American friend, the foster father decided to teach James a lesson about what he believed was an improper mixing of races. "He hit me, my head tilted forward and I saw my blood splotch my crisp, white socks."

James screamed as his foster father dragged him outside and handcuffed him to the pole of the family's confederate flag. "I heard my scream fade and all that

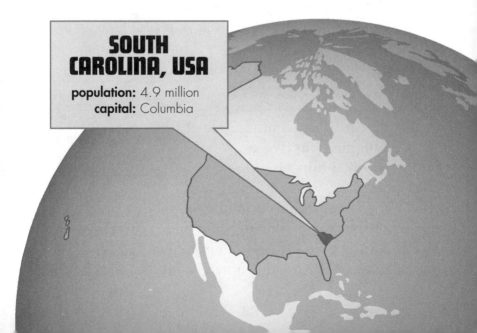

SOUTH CAROLINA, USA
population: 4.9 million
capital: Columbia

was left was a ringing silence. I knew no one would come to help, so there was no use in calling for it," James writes. It was a cold December night, and James wasn't wearing clothes. He spent the night, hand-cuffed to the flagpole.

When the foster family lost their fostering license due to another charge of abuse, James moved back into a group home.

Having experienced the worst of the foster care system, James decided he wanted to change it. After graduating with top grades from South Carolina University at age 19, he spent a summer in Washington, D.C., working for congressmen Mick Mulvaney and Joe Wilson. When he was 21 years old, James graduated from the University of Southern California (USC) with a master's degree in social work.

"Growing up in the foster care system, I was con-stantly told I would never amount to anything. Like a plant, I could have allowed it to stunt my growth. But I had a choice. I could either flourish despite the odds or fall through the cracks in the system," he says in a video he made while he was a student at USC.

"Sometimes that's just the way it is in foster care. So what are you going to do from there? And it comes down to what is your future, what do you want in life, and how are you going to get that?" he says.

Now, he is the director of business development at Echoes of Hope, a nonprofit that works to empower foster children. Soon, he wants to go back to school to earn his Ph.D. in child welfare policy.

"At the end of the day, there are many foster youth that aren't being served. At the end of the day, these foster youth are realizing they have to rely on themselves. They have to rely on their resiliency," James says. "They realize they can't be a victim anymore. They have to be a victor."

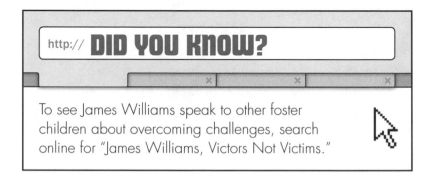

http:// **DID YOU KNOW?**

To see James Williams speak to other foster children about overcoming challenges, search online for "James Williams, Victors Not Victims."

That Girl in Pink
Benni Cinkle

Believe it or not, there was a time before video streaming—back when dinosaurs roamed the earth and the worst place you could have your most embarrassing moment was in front of your whole school. How many people would see it? Maybe a couple hundred? A thousand at most? You could still move to another city, change your name, and pretend to be someone new who hadn't actually done that totally embarrassing thing. But what do you do when your most awkward moment is seen by 70 million people? Enter the power of the Internet: With just a little bad luck, your most embarrassing moment can be filmed, uploaded, go viral, and, at least for a couple minutes, become more popular than kittens falling off shelves.

That's what happened to Benni Cinkle. She was in the music video for the song "Friday" by her friend, Rebecca Black. Sounds pretty cool, huh? Well, after the video, Benni Cinkle became known as "the awkward girl dancing next to Rebecca Black." To be honest, her dancing is a bit awkward. Of the 70 million people who watched Benni Cinkle's embarrassing moment, thousands and thousands of them lit up the Internet with mean comments about her dancing.

People wrote, "Is this the girl on the video with the huge mole?" and, "I never knew awkward dancing could be as awkward as the girl in the pink dress. Bahaha!" In her infamous dance, Benni kind of waves her hands back and forth in the air. Someone made a clip of the video and magically added an accordion and a mustache so it looks like Benni is playing along with the song. There's no sugar coating it: It's horrendously embarrassing.

Cinkle's response? She made her own video introducing herself to all the haters.

In her video she says, "The producers told me to be silly and weird so I was just like, um, okay? I didn't really know what that meant. So I was just weird, and this [dance] just kind of came out so they put it in."

Benni is humble, charming, honest, and real—exactly the opposite of the people writing mean comments. She says the accordion clip is her favorite. And she says that now one of the most common questions people ask her online is if she will marry them. In her video, she says, "I just want to say that yes, I will marry you. I will in fact marry you. All of you."

All of a sudden, the comments changed to things like "This girl is an awkward form of WIN," and, "If only all Internet nonsense was handled this way!"

Benni didn't stop at a video. She started the That Girl in Pink Foundation to fight cyberbullying. She speaks about bullying at schools. And she wrote an Internet Survival Guide that included advice like, "Surviving life on the Internet is about being okay with who you are, quirks and all," and says that after the music video, she had two choices: "I could take things personally and feel bad, or I could not take things personally and not feel bad."

Benni Cinkle chose not to feel bad. And by being resilient enough to be herself, she has helped thousands of people around the world feel a little better about themselves, too.

CALIFORNIA, USA

population: 39.1 million
capital: Sacramento

Music from the Heart
Diego Frazão Torquato

In Brazil, over 11 million people live in slums called *favelas*. That's like the entire population of the state of Ohio living in ramshackle houses and apartments packed together like wooden building blocks thrown willy-nilly onto a playroom floor. Instead of following the laws of the Brazilian government, many of the country's *favelas* follow the laws of drug gangs, who rule with fear and intimidation. In these slums, there is the danger of violence from the gangs, and there is also the danger of *joining* the gangs. Many children born in the *favelas* join groups of drug traffickers who move drugs, like cocaine, from where they are grown to where they are sold and used.

One of these *favelas,* located near Rio de Janeiro, is called Parada de Lucas.

Not much is known about Parada de Lucas. When you search online for the name, you might find an extremely short Wikipedia description and an article in Portuguese titled *"Fronteiras do Trafico"* ("Frontiers of Trafficking"). You might also find a few pictures showing things like Brazilian police in bullet-proof vests conducting raids with guns, soldiers aiming assault rifles from the back of a flatbed truck, and views across rooftops that seem to point in all directions and no direction at once.

Searching for Parada de Lucas also returns the picture of a boy of African descent crying while he plays the violin. This is Diego Frazão Torquato. The picture was taken at the funeral of his violin teacher. In the picture, Diego's violin and the tear streaming from his right eye have the same shine.

Diego did not have an easy life. In the Parada de Lucas *favela* where he was born, the drug traffickers weren't the only reason the neighborhood was dangerous. It was also a place where kids caught diseases that are uncommon in areas of the world with better sanitation and medical care. When Diego was four, he caught meningitis, a disease that creates swelling around the brain and spinal cord. Due to the illness, Diego had memory problems. But that didn't stop him from learning to play the violin.

When he was six years old, he started taking classes at a nonprofit organization called AfroReggae, which taught kids from the *favelas* about Brazilian culture through soccer, drumming, dance, graffiti art, and the Brazilian dance-fighting called *capoeira*. The organization hoped that by involving young people in these activities, it would keep them from joining the gangs of drug traffickers. AfroReggae also had an orchestra, which was led by Evandro João da Silva. Evandro became more than Diego's teacher—Evandro was a mentor and almost like a father to Diego.

Diego never learned to read music, but he played by ear and practiced hard. With Evandro and the AfroReggae Orchestra, Diego played concerts and even played on Brazilian television shows. In a video of one of these concerts, you can see Diego standing in the front line of violins. He's a head taller than everyone else and smiles while he plays. The group plays

BRAZIL
population: 200 million
capital: Brasília

a medley of classical tunes mixed with American pop songs, but there's no doubt it's fully *Brazilian:* In the hands of the AfroReggae Orchestra, even the classical music of Mozart has a bit of a Brazilian samba swing that makes you want to dance.

"Today I am an artist," Diego says in the video. He wears his joy on his face.

The AfroReggae Orchestra became a symbol of hope for the people of Brazil's *favelas.* Diego showed that it was possible to overcome the ugliness of poverty, disease, violence, and drug trafficking to create something beautiful. His music touched people's hearts.

On October 18, 2009, Diego's teacher, Evandro, was shot to death. The murder was caught on a surveillance camera: Two thugs threw Evandro to the ground, shot him, and took his coat. Then a police car drove by. Instead of helping Evandro, the car chased the thieves. The police caught the thieves . . . and then let them go. Later, the police officers returned to take Evandro's belongings and left Evandro to bleed to death.

It was all so unfair. That is why Diego is crying in the famous photograph.

Diego's life had not been easy before his teacher's death, and it was not easy after, either. In January 2010, he began feeling ill. When he visited the hospital, he was diagnosed with appendicitis, a swelling of the appendix that can be life-threatening if it's not treated right away. But even after having his appendix removed, Diego didn't recover. It turned out that what looked like an infection in his appendix was something else entirely: Diego had leukemia, a type of blood cancer. By that point, he was already so sick that his body couldn't withstand the powerful treatment for the disease.

Diego died a week later. He was 12 years old.

Here is what the new leader of AffroReggae said at Diego's funeral: "I think the legacy of Diego is hope, it is the willingness to change, to transform."

Diego lived a short and difficult life. But during that time, he brought the world joy.

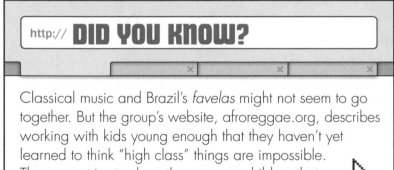

http:// **DID YOU KNOW?**

Classical music and Brazil's *favelas* might not seem to go together. But the group's website, afroreggae.org, describes working with kids young enough that they haven't yet learned to think "high class" things are impossible. The group tries to show these young children that possibilities exist before they stop believing.

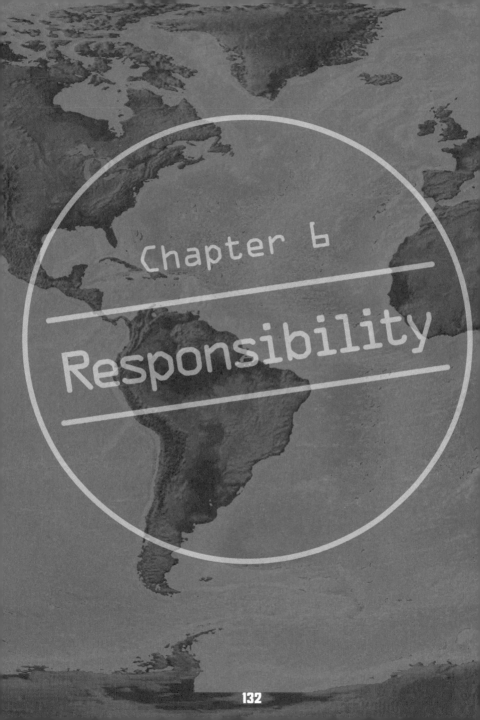

Chapter 6

Responsibility

A baseball player admits that he was tagged out. A girl returns a wallet she finds on the bus. A teenager cleans a wall where his friends painted graffiti. These are examples of responsibility, right? They sure are. But there's another side to responsibility: taking responsibility to make positive changes for the world, other people, or even for yourself.

When you look out at the world, it's easy to imagine that it's someone else's job to make things better. There are people in charge of everything from picking up garbage to making new laws. When a street light goes out, there's a person responsible for changing it. And people like teachers, coaches, social workers, and doctors are responsible for other people. There are probably people who are responsible for *you*—without help, would you get to school on time, with both shoes on your feet?

Maybe the answer to this last question is yes. At least, that's the answer for many of the young people in this section. In addition to things like giving back wallets, the people in this section take responsibility for themselves, others, or for change in their communities. Some are forced into responsibility and some seek it out. Like the kids in this section, try asking yourself, "If not me, then who?"

Tower of Power
William Kamkwamba

William Kamkwamba lived in the African country of Malawi. When he was 13 years old, the country was deep in the middle of a drought. There was no rain. No rain meant no crops. No crops meant no money. And no money meant that William's family couldn't afford to send him to school.

So he decided to take responsibility for his own education. An aid organization had built a tiny library in his village, and William started going every day. He couldn't read English very well, so he spent most of his time looking at pictures. One of these pictures was of a windmill used to generate electricity.

His village didn't have electricity—people used batteries to charge cell phones and made do without things like lights and fans. It would have been great if the same aid organization that built the library had also built a power station. But instead of waiting for that to happen, William decided to take responsibility for the power station himself. He would build a windmill. The other people in his village thought he was crazy.

"I may be crazy, but this picture in this book means that somebody somewhere did this," he said.

After looking at the picture, William went to Home Depot and RadioShack and bought the supplies he needed to make the windmill. Just kidding. There was no Home Depot and no RadioShack, and William didn't have money to buy pieces, anyway. Instead, he scrounged things from rusty bikes, an old tractor, and broken electronics.

The crux of the problem was how to use the wind to turn an electric motor. When you send electricity into a motor, it turns the shaft. Or when you use some other sort of power to turn the shaft, it sends electricity out. William's windmill would use the strength of the wind to turn an electric motor, which would create electricity.

The first step was to reach up into the wind. He built a tall, pyramid-shaped frame with three, 15-foot blue gum trees. For windmill blades, he used flattened PVC pipe attached to sticks of bamboo. He mounted these blades to a rusty, circular fan he salvaged from an old tractor. The shaft of the fan drove a bike tire, whose gear drove a rubber belt, which ran through pulleys and turned the electric motor. From the motor, long copper wires ran down from the windmill and into a car battery in the corner of William's house. Put it all together, and the energy of the wind charged the battery.

Of course, there were problems. One of these problems came from the fact that electricity can act like a mob of people rushing a gate at a concert. When electricity rushes the gate, things go bad.

"After I built the windmill, I noticed that I needed a circuit breaker," William said. A circuit breaker is a device that stands guard over an electric system, ready to turn the whole thing off immediately if something goes haywire. A circuit breaker meant that when things went wrong (and William knew that things were *bound* to go wrong), the windmill wouldn't create

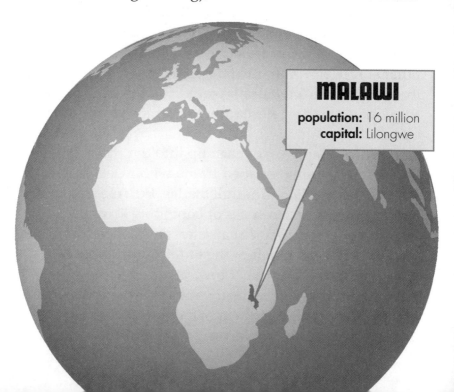

MALAWI
population: 16 million
capital: Lilongwe

all sorts of badness like blowing up and burning down his house and village. That's something William *didn't* want to be responsible for.

In his village's small lending library, he found an American eighth-grade textbook titled *Using Energy.* He still couldn't read English, but William looked at the pictures, taught himself to interpret some of the electrical diagrams, and then improvised the best he could. His circuit breaker was an open box about the size of the palm of your hand. Nails were hammered into the side walls so that the heads of the nails almost touched in the center of the box. Between the nail heads was a magnet. The shafts of the nails were wrapped with thin copper wire. The current from the windmill flowed through the wires from one side to the other. If something went wrong and too much current flowed through the wires, it would pull the magnet away from the center and "break" the circuit. Just like snipping the battery wire on an electric toy, if the current couldn't go through the circuit breaker, the whole thing turned off.

Now instead of burning down his house, William used the windmill to light his house with electricity. The current he generated was enough to power four light bulbs, a radio, and charge neighbors' mobile phones. (You can bet they didn't think he was crazy anymore.)

But he kept working to make things better. It was great to be able to flip a switch and have a light come on, but the biggest problem in his village wasn't lights—it was the lack of water to use for growing crops. Surely someone would do something about the village's water problem? Again, William decided not to wait for that "someone" to come along. Instead, he took responsibility for that task himself. William built another windmill, double the height of the first one so it caught more wind above the trees, and he rigged it to pump used water from people's houses out into the fields to grow crops.

You probably have electricity and running water. But like William, you can probably see things in the world that you wish were different. Whose responsibility is it to change these things? Is it "someone" . . . or is it you?

http:// **DID YOU KNOW?**

You can see William Kamkwamba's talk "How I Built a Windmill" at ted.com.

Around the World in 519 Days

Laura Dekker

Laura Dekker was born on a sailboat off the coast of New Zealand. For the first five years of her life, she woke up with the sun rising from the blue horizon and slept with the motion of the waves aboard the family's small boat, the *Guppy*. As much as the ocean could flow through a person's veins, it flowed through Laura's. The ocean was what she knew and what she loved.

A small sailboat can be confining, though, and it wasn't always easy for Laura's family to live in such close quarters. Eventually her parents divorced, and Laura moved with her father to his home country, the Netherlands, where he took a job in a boatyard. Laura's father bought her a tiny dinghy, which she learned to sail while her father windsurfed alongside. For her eighth birthday, Laura's father gave her

a book titled *Maiden Voyage*. The book told the story
of American sailor Tania Aebi's solo trip around the
world. Eight-year-old Laura started dreaming.

Along with her dreams, Laura's trips got more
ambitious. By the time she was nine, she was bor-
rowing a friend's 20-foot sailboat, which she sailed
by herself along the Dutch coast. Laura started doing
longer solo trips during summer vacations and made a
solo crossing to England when she was 13.

At age 14, Laura started doing more than dreaming. She started planning. With a loan from her
father, Laura bought her own sailboat, a 40-foot ketch
she named *Guppy* after the original family boat in
New Zealand.

In late August 2010, 14-year-old Laura set out all
by herself to sail around the world, starting in Den
Osse in the Netherlands. The Dutch government
tried to stop her, saying it was too risky. They had a
point. Just a couple months earlier, another teenage
solo sailor, Abby Sunderland, had sailed from Marina
del Rey in California, trying to become the youngest
person to circumnavigate the world in a sailboat by
herself. Unfortunately, Abby was hit by a storm in the
southern Indian Ocean, halfway between Australia
and Africa. The storm ripped the mast off her ship and
disabled her communication system. Abby activated a
rescue beacon and after a massive search, was picked
up by a French fishing boat. Her sailboat, the *Wild
Eyes*, was left to sink.

Laura's parents knew the ocean and understood the risks. Her parents also felt like the modern world was overprotective. They felt like Laura should be allowed to learn through independence and sometimes danger. In the end, Laura was allowed to go. Laura brought a video camera with her and talked to it along the way. In the movie *Maidentrip,* made from her footage, you can see Laura cut off her long blond hair and dye it red. She learns to cook. She yells at the big waves that crash over her bow. She turns 15 and then 16. She stands at the helm of the *Guppy* with blue-green waves to the horizon, a sun-streak in the east, and the shadow of the mast to the west. She says good morning to the breeze.

And she is completely alone, responsible for decisions and actions that make the difference between life and death. One of these decisions was whether to risk pirates in the northern Indian Ocean off the northeast coast of Africa or turn south to go around the southern

THE NETHERLANDS

population: 16.8 million
capital: Amsterdam

tip of Africa in notoriously dangerous seas. Laura weighed the decision, made up her own mind, and chose stormy seas over piracy.

The Cape of Good Hope, at the southern tip of South Africa, used to be known by sailors as the Cape of Storms. When sailing around the world, you can skip other dangerous places. For example, instead of sailing around Cape Horn at the southern tip of South America, you can cut through the Panama Canal. And if you pick the right season, you're not likely to end up drifting in the Indian Ocean, like Abby Sunderland. But unless you risk pirates, there's nothing you can do about the Cape of Good Hope. There's no way around it, and it's almost certain to be a wild ride.

On her little camera, you can see Laura rounding the Cape of Good Hope. The swells are gigantic, big enough to make the *Guppy* look like the cars you see far below from an airplane window. In a storm, sailors drop the main sail so that high winds don't blow the boat over and rip apart the mast. Rounding the Cape of Good Hope, Laura put up her storm jib, a smaller sail that lets her maneuver the boat without giving the winds enough of a target to turn the sailboat into a broken kite.

In the night, the winds got so strong that even the storm jib was too much. But it was jammed! Laura couldn't get it down, and with the sail up, the wind blew the little boat like you would blow a feather. Who would save her? Would it be a French fishing boat, like Abby Sunderland? Or her parents, or another sailboat, or the Coast Guard, or a prince riding in on some sort of white seahorse? In a storm like that, the answer was nobody—nobody but herself was going to save her.

"I didn't feel anything but focused. Being scared was totally gone. I didn't feel that I was hungry or tired. I was just doing it," Laura said in her voice diary.

Eventually, just before sunrise, Laura was able to pull down the storm jib and round the Cape of Good Hope. At that point in the video, you can see that she goes from a girl on an adventure to the confident skipper of her solo voyage around the world. You can see Laura own her life and take full responsibility for her choices.

After 519 days and 27,000 nautical miles, Laura landed in Simpson Bay at the Caribbean island St. Maarten, the official endpoint of her voyage. Looking back, 16-year-old Laura said in her voice diary, "I wanted the storms. I wanted the calms. I wanted to feel loneliness. And now I know all these things. It's the end of the dream I had as a kid, and it's the beginning of my life as a sailor."

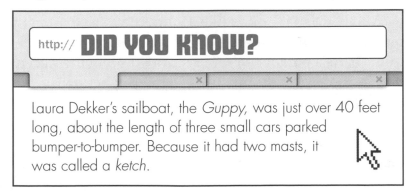

http:// **DID YOU KNOW?**

Laura Dekker's sailboat, the *Guppy*, was just over 40 feet long, about the length of three small cars parked bumper-to-bumper. Because it had two masts, it was called a *ketch*.

Jailed for Responsibility
Diane Tran

In this story about responsibility, you might have to decide what is responsible and what is not. First, let's meet the protagonist.

In 2012, Diane Tran was a junior at Willis High School in Houston, Texas, and the daughter of immigrants from Vietnam. She was an honors student taking AP Spanish, college-level algebra, and classes in English and history that earned both high school and college credits.

Maybe Diane sounds like a student whose parents pushed her too hard, but actually, the opposite was true. Diane's parents were so wrapped up in their own problems they pretty much let Diane run her own life. During her junior year, they went a step further. Diane's parents split up and moved away, leaving Diane completely on her own. It wasn't only Diane that her parents left—Diane had an older brother who was going to school at Texas A&M University, and a younger sister who stayed with relatives in Houston. Now without a real home, Diane slept at one of her two jobs.

That's right, Diane had *two jobs*—she worked full time at a dry cleaners and part time at a wedding venue. This meant that in addition to school, Diane was working about 60 hours every week. She used the money she made to support her brother and sister.

"She goes from job to job from school. She stays up until 7:00 in the morning doing her homework," one of her friends told a local TV station.

There's no doubt Diane was a hero. But here's where her story gets a little complicated. As you can

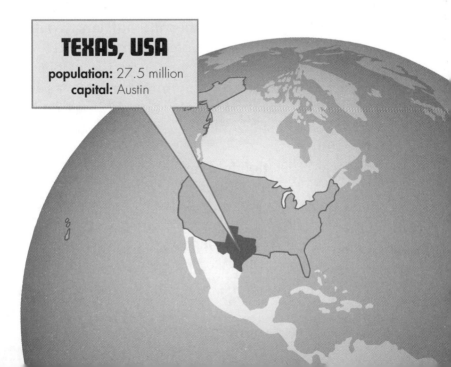

TEXAS, USA
population: 27.5 million
capital: Austin

imagine, Diane didn't always make it to school on time. Some days, she didn't make it to school at all. Texas law says that if you have more than 10 unexcused absences in six months, the school can send you to court. In April 2012, that's what happened to Diane. In court, the judge warned her not to miss any more school.

Diane continued to work. She continued to study. But the responsibility she felt to earn money to support her brother and sister meant that she also missed more school.

In May 2012, she was back in court. This time, the judge came down hard, saying that if he let one kid skip school, he would have to let them all. He ordered Diane to spend 24 hours in jail and to pay a $100 fine. Even worse, the punishment meant that Diane would have a mark on her permanent record that would make it harder to get into college or earn the scholarships she needed to pay for it. Remember, she was an honors student working to support her siblings, and now it looked like she would pay for these good deeds with her future!

The local TV station told her story. Newspapers as far away as London, England, wrote about what happened. The Internet lit up with support for Diane. More than 35,000 people signed a petition asking the judge to clear Diane's record and reverse the $100 fine. It worked! The judge couldn't take back the 24 hours Diane had spent in jail, but at least he wiped her record clean so Diane wouldn't have to admit she'd been to jail when she applied to colleges.

Now it's your turn to decide what was the "responsible" thing to do. Was Diane acting responsibly, earning money for her siblings at the expense of her education? Or was she acting irresponsibly, missing school to the point that she put her future at risk? If you were Diane, what would you have done?

http:// **DID YOU KNOW?**

With a quick online search for Diane Tran's name, you can watch the touching, heartfelt video she made to thank her supporters.

A School of One
Sarbast Ali

When Sarbast Ali was three years old, an illness stole the use of his legs. Neither Sarbast nor his family knew the name of the disease, only that one week he could use his legs and the next week he could not. What do three-year-olds do? They adapt! Living in the Syrian city of Damascus, Sarbast started school just like any other kid. The streets were paved and safe. At first, his father pushed him to school, and when he was old enough, Sarbast learned to roll his wheelchair from the family's apartment to school himself.

Then civil war came to Syria. The government of Syria had been telling people what they could and couldn't say, and a group of rebels decided to fight for their freedom. The government fought back. They cut off the supply of food to areas where the rebels lived. Sarbast's family lived in one of these neighborhoods.

"The situation went from bad to worse in Damascus. War was coming to the suburbs, there wasn't enough food, and everyone was scared, so we left our home," 13-year-old Sarbast told the international aid organization UNICEF.

They weren't alone. During the Syrian civil war, 6.5 million people were forced to leave their homes to live somewhere else within the country. Another 3 million people left the country entirely, fleeing to Turkey, Lebanon, Jordan, and Iraq. Some of these people found apartments in cities and jobs to support their families. Those who couldn't afford apartments lived in refugee camps.

Sarbast's family fled to Northern Iraq. His father, Loqman, had to carry Sarbast two miles across the border. Eventually, they arrived at the Domiz Refugee Camp, a tent city of 45,000 people built in the dirt with white canvas and blue plastic tarps.

"I was not happy when I arrived at Domiz camp. It was madness and crowds, and we had to live with another family for the first two months. Every day I was asking my father when we would go back to Syria. I didn't think we would stay here," Sarbast says.

But eventually, it became clear that Domiz was more than a quick vacation—at least for now, it was home. For Sarbast, his six brothers and sisters, and the other thousands of children in the camp, that meant going to school. In the Domiz camp, there was a rectangular school built from cinder blocks, but Sarbast couldn't get from his tent to the school across the rough ground.

Rather than falling behind, Sarbast decided to take his education into his own hands. He had an old laptop computer, and even though the camp struggled to provide clean water and medical care, it did have electricity and Internet access. That was all Sarbast needed. He downloaded a program that helped him learn to speak English. He downloaded science lessons from National Geographic Learning "because I want to collect information on everything," he says. When his friends in the camp went to school, Sarbast studied in his tent.

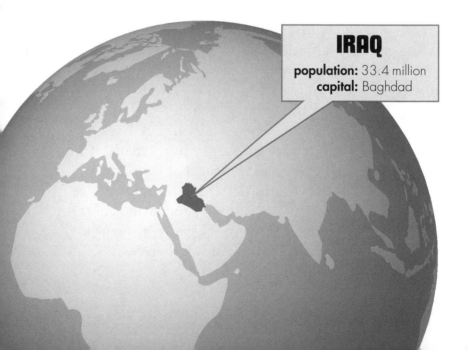

IRAQ
population: 33.4 million
capital: Baghdad

Sarbast hoped that one day he would be able to leave the Domiz refugee camp and go back to a regular school. Maybe then he could receive medical treatment or at least a definite diagnosis for the illness that paralyzed his legs. Maybe one day he could become a pilot! Until then, Sarbast would do the best he could, taking responsibility for his own education even if that meant doing it on his own.

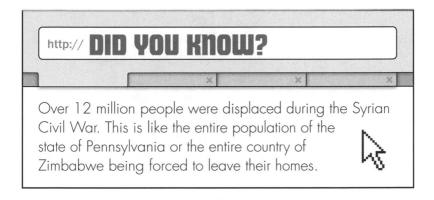

http:// **DID YOU KNOW?**

Over 12 million people were displaced during the Syrian Civil War. This is like the entire population of the state of Pennsylvania or the entire country of Zimbabwe being forced to leave their homes.

A NOTE FROM THE AUTHOR

While I was writing this book, I started to think about character like a cake recipe: two cups of courage, three tablespoons of creativity, a cup of kindness, and just a pinch of persistence, bake for 30 minutes at 375 degrees and there you have it! Unfortunately, I'm a terrible cook. I can set off the smoke alarm while making a bowl of cereal. So for me, this recipe for character started to seem a little overwhelming. How could I remember to act with courage, while also being kind and persistent and creative? It seemed like a lot of pressure and a lot of things to remember.

However, another thing I came to believe after writing this book is that the voice of character lives inside every human being. You may not know how to bake a cake, but if you listen closely to your heart, it will tell you how to act with character. Maybe this character comes out as creativity or maybe it's courage or maybe it's resilience, but what character looks like doesn't matter nearly as much as the choice to listen to your heart's voice. It will tell you how to act. When you listen, *that's* character.

Really, that's all the people in this book did. They aren't comic book superheroes who happened to be born with the power of character. They are no different from you. They have the same "amount" of character that you have. Only, when a situation came along and their character spoke to them, they chose to listen.

You can listen, too. Try it today. Try it right now. When you look at the challenges in your life, the lives of the people you care about, or the world around you, what does the voice of character inside of you say? Can you hear it? Now, the recipe for character is easy: Just listen to what you know is right.

If you have stories about young people showing character, I would love to hear them. You can write to me at:

Garth Sundem
c/o Free Spirit Publishing
6325 Sandburg Road, Suite 100
Minneapolis, MN 55427-3674

Or you can email me: help4kids@freespirit.com

INDEX

ABOUT THE AUTHOR

Garth Sundem enjoys speaking about the power of character and has written several books for teachers and kids, including *Real Kids, Real Stories, Real Change.* He has pursued interests including rock climbing and music and, after living in many different countries, now calls Boulder, Colorado, home.

Also by Garth
Real Kids, Real Stories, Real Change
Courageous Actions
Around the World
For ages 9–13
*176 pp.; 2-color; paperback; 5¼" x 7½"
ISBN 978-1-57542-350-0*